Divorce Without Victims

Divorce Without Victims

Helping Children Through Divorce
with a Minimum of Pain and Trauma

Stuart Berger, M.D.

Boston

HOUGHTON MIFFLIN COMPANY

1983

Library of Congress Cataloging in Publication Data
Berger, Stuart.
Divorce without victims.

1. Children of divorced parents—United States.
2. Divorced parents—United States. 3. Parent and child—
United States. I. Title.
HQ777.5.B46   1983   306.8'9'0973   82–15680
ISBN 0–395–33115–3

This book is dedicated to
the welfare of future generations
and to the memory of
my grandmother Anna, whose love
was for children.

Contents

Acknowledgments

Many people have contributed — each in a unique way — to the successful completion of this book. All have given generously of their time, their expertise, and their emotional support. I would like to thank them now, publicly, for their help. I will be always in their debt.

Mrs. Albert D. Lasker's intelligent criticism and persuasive comments resulted, in good part, in what I hope is the fairly readable tone of this book. Mrs. Lasker lobbied unceasingly against the use of incomprehensible psychiatric jargon and for the use of Standard American English. Her efforts will have made this book infinitely more useful to parents.

Geraldine Stutz constantly provided new insights into the complicated issues that are the subject of this book, thereby enriching me, personally, and the book's treatment of these issues.

Leonard Bernstein, Betty Comden, Barbara Gordon, and Susan Kasen all provided me with much-needed encouragement and support throughout the long, sometimes difficult period spanning my work on this project.

Over the last few years I had the good fortune to work with Charles McGowan, Director of the Youth Coliseum of Project Return. Project Return is a facility for abused or neglected children. During the years I worked there, Charles's example taught me a great deal about what it means to act with humanity toward children.

I have also had the privilege of working with Dr. Anthony Atwell of the Child Custody Clinic of Stanford University. During my months at Stanford, Dr. Atwell proved invaluable as a teacher and as a friend.

Dr. Nathan Kline was kind enough to review the manuscript while it was in progress and to offer his own insights and thoughts.

I would particularly like to thank Dr. Myles Schneider, a colleague and friend, whose great expertise, offered always with kindness and humor, helped me to sort out my thinking on nearly every aspect of the complicated relationships between divorced parents and their children.

I am indebted also to Mary Libroia, my secretary, for helping with the production of the manuscript and — especially — for tolerating my moodiness whenever I had to confront a particularly difficult problem or issue. Linda Lane not only typed most of the manuscript but also offered insights based on her own knowledge of this field.

Most particularly, I want to thank Anne Lopatto, friend and editor, for her skillful and painstaking editing of this manuscript. Anne's help in organizing this book and in overseeing my prose style was invaluable.

My last, and most important, acknowledgment must go to my parents, Rachel and Otto Berger, whose hard work and self-lessness made my education possible, and whose compassion and humor help me keep my work and my life in healthy perspective.

Introduction
Your Child and Divorce

It has been estimated that at least one million children in this country are involved in divorce proceedings *every year*. It has also been estimated that one half of all American marriages now in existence will end in divorce.

Whether or not these statistics prove a basic crisis in American society or a basic failure of one of our most valued institutions is for others to decide. But what is indisputable is that many millions of children are being, and will be, subjected to the considerable stress and anxiety that accompany the separation and divorce of their parents.

Children are remarkably resilient creatures, and it is by no means inevitable that the separation or divorce of their parents will leave them with permanent psychological scars. Often, however, divorcing parents are themselves in so troubled and emotional a state that they either foster exaggerated fears for their child's welfare or ignore the child's early warning signals of troubled behavior.

But, by becoming acquainted with certain fundamental principles relating to the workings of a child's mind, parents can take an enormous step in helping the child through this difficult period. That is one purpose of this book. The second, and equally central purpose, is to help parents understand how their own feelings and actions influence the progress of the child during and after the divorce. Finally, the book attempts to outline certain of those situations in which the child may need the benefit of professional therapy or counseling.

Even during the trauma of divorce, two genuinely loving parents can be of inestimable help to their children. The effective expression of underlying parent-child love can, in this critical period, help both parent and child to grow.

Stuart Berger, M.D.

Divorce Without Victims

1

The Mind of the Child

AMONG MY GRAMMAR SCHOOL CLASSMATES in Brooklyn, not quite twenty years ago, divorce was a rare and mysterious event. In that heavily ethnic blue-collar community, "Till death do us part" was more than an empty ceremonial phrase; it was part of a solemn vow. Marriage lasted forever; the very idea of divorce was associated not only with social disgrace but with religious and personal failure. Parents did not feel comfortable even discussing the subject in front of their children, let alone presenting it as a normal or understandable occurrence.

Perhaps that's why we third-graders viewed our two classmates whose parents had been divorced with such a mixture of awe and pity. We all knew that Eddie and Tom came from "broken homes"; schoolyard gossip had seen to that. We also knew, though we did not really understand, some of the details behind these neighborhood scandals.

Eddie's mother, it was whispered, had actually packed her bags and left her husband and three children when Eddie was still in kindergarten. Though none of us knew anything of the actual reasons behind her departure, we assumed that only an unnatural or "bad" mother would do such an unthinkable thing. Certainly it was something our own mothers would not — or perhaps, could not — explain to us. Those of us who asked were told that it was none of our business, or "nothing for children to hear." We did know that Eddie now lived with his father, his two older brothers, and with someone called his stepmother. The only stepmothers we had ever heard about were those in fairy tales. Fairy-tale stepmothers, of course, were uniformly cruel and ugly and treated their stepchildren badly. We all felt sorry for Eddie because he had to put up with such a person, and we guardedly examined the offending stepmother — who was probably a perfectly pleasant woman — whenever we saw her.

Tom had a stepmother, too, though he lived with his "real" mother and her new husband. Nobody seemed to know the reason why Tom's parents had been divorced, though occasionally we heard that Tom's father "had problems" or that he couldn't hold down a job. But we all thought it very odd that Tom should have two sets of parents, and we wondered among ourselves which set would turn up on Parents' Night, or to see the school play.

I understand now that my parents and my classmates' parents were trying to shield us from what they regarded as an unpleasant, and unusual, fact of life. But I wish, for all our sakes — theirs, Eddie's, Tom's, mine — that our parents had openly discussed and explained divorce to us third-graders. Instead, we were left to grapple with our fantasies and our fears. The thought of a mother who just "walked out" on our classmate Eddie, for example, was a terrifying one to us eight-year-olds. It raised all sorts of fears: "Would our mothers walk out on us, too, if we behaved badly? What had Eddie done to deserve this? How could we avoid a similar fate? What exactly was involved in a divorce, anyway, and how did such a thing happen?" Because we really knew nothing about the reason for divorce, or the divorce process itself, we felt we had no control over it: It was just something that happened to a child, like being struck by lightning. The very thought of having to live in what was always called a broken home seemed particularly horrible to us. Our obvious feelings of fear, pity, and curiosity must have been realized by Eddie and Tom. No wonder both boys seemed so quiet and tentative.

Things are very different in the 1980s. In today's grammar schools, including religious-affiliated schools, divorce seems almost commonplace. With one million children involved in divorce proceedings every year, divorce has come out of the classroom closet and ostentatiously taken its place in the very first row. Children of divorce are not social freaks or pariahs; indeed, in certain urban classrooms they almost seem to outnumber their peers whose parents aren't divorced.

For the last two decades, certain experts have been predicting that the traditional nuclear family — two once-and-forever-married adults who together raise their biological children to maturity — may soon be a thing of the past. The 1960s, for example, saw many much-publicized attempts at communal living. The more radical of these communal groups experimented with so-called group marriage. These arrangements, which of course are not legally recognized as marriages, commonly provided that every man in the commune was considered "married" to every communal woman, and vice versa. Many such groups also provided that every adult in the group was fully a parent to every child born into its community.

This lifestyle did not live up to its enthusiastic publicity; it certainly had little impact on the fate of the nuclear family in the United States. This is not surprising, when one realizes that communes of various sorts have appeared regularly in this country throughout the last two centuries of our history, and they have always been short-lived.

But if communal living did nothing to change the traditional family unit, with its long-held moral and social values, the recent escalation of divorce *has* done a very great deal. If the prediction that half of all American marriages now in existence will eventually be terminated by divorce, the result will be millions of single-parent households, millions of children being raised by a stepparent, millions of siblings being raised apart from one another. The implications for our society are staggering. Divorce has accomplished what a radical counterculture movement of the 60s could not: It has changed the face — and the values — of American society.

The Eddies and the Toms in today's grammar schools, then, don't have to endure as much negative attention from their classmates as they would have two decades ago; but this does not mean that today's children of divorce will not face problems. These problems are apt to stem from the divorce itself rather than from social stigma or peer ridicule. And in too many cases, such problems will be worsened by the behavior of one or both divorcing parents.

If I could abolish one phrase from the English language, it would be *broken home,* a term used far too often, thoughtlessly and automatically, to describe the condition of *every* child whose parents have been divorced. And it is a phrase that, quite incorrectly, implies that every child of divorced parents is doomed to a life of psychological illness, drug dependence, or alcoholism, or equally serious problems. Every divorced parent who hears the words *broken home* must, if only for a second, fight down nightmarish images of juvenile delinquency, school failure, or worse.

Ironically, even with divorce becoming a commonplace, there are few places for parents to turn to receive sound advice on helping their child during and after the divorce. Undoubtedly, the divorce will prove very difficult for a child to understand and accept. After all, marital separation and divorce are traumatic events, for adults as well as children. Yet it is also true that knowledgeable and caring parents can do much to help the child understand and, eventually, accept the new living situation.

To do this most effectively, however, it is important that the parents understand how a child sees the world. No matter how attentive or loving parents are, they cannot be expected to act as mindreaders, magically guessing their children's every thought and fear. All children pass through many intellectual and emotional stages of growth, stages that can greatly affect their ability to understand and accept an event as important as parental divorce.

Understandably, there are many parents who resent the very notion of consulting so-called experts or handbooks for advice on child rearing. One young father recently stated — very emphatically — a view that is often heard. "I don't need any books to help me raise my own kids. I love them. I've watched them grow. I understand them. Besides," he finished heatedly, "I was a kid myself, not so terribly long ago. I remember what being a kid was like."

This young father was largely right. His love and consistent attention to his children had nurtured in him a very highly developed sensitivity to their needs. What's more, such sensitivity is invaluable and irreplaceable in a parent. Without it, both parent and child will find the child's growing years extremely difficult and even estranging. But it's also true that parents can add to their appreciation of their child's experience by familiarizing themselves with some of the basic concepts of child development and child psychology. While all parents have, as our young father pointed out, "been kids themselves," it is impossible for adults to truly reconstruct their total childhood experience. Indeed, most of us have no memory at all of our very earliest years, which are crucial to the child's emotional development. Ordinarily, our earliest memories date from about the age of two, and even these are incomplete and fragmented. Actually, our memories of later years cannot be relied on as entirely accurate.

In fact, one of the more interesting controversies currently raging in psychiatry has to do with the very nature of memory. Some experts now hold firmly to the view that a memory is not, as most of us think, a fixed, "true" picture of an event. They hold that this notion of an objective, unchanging memory is either retrieved ("remembered") or lost ("forgotten"). Memories, they say, may change from year to year, or even day to day. They may also change according to our emotional state; that is, according to what we *want* or *need* to remember.

Actual examples of this phenomenon are fairly common, as any psychiatrist knows. Ken, a successful young musician, had one very unhappy memory, which he confided to only his closest friends. When he was eight years old, Ken said, he had been climbing a tree in his back yard and had spotted a bird's nest in the upper branches. Excited and eager to see if any baby birds were in the nest, Ken climbed as far up the tree as he dared. In doing so, he accidentally knocked the bird's nest to the ground, killing the two tiny birds within.

What was startling was Ken's memory of the consequences of this accident. Ken recalled — and had told his friends — that his mother had witnessed the incident and, furious about his "bad" behavior, had screamed at him and even struck him. More than two decades later, at the age of thirty, Ken still became visibly upset whenever he recounted this story.

But Ken's memory was highly inaccurate. The truth, as a friend found out quite accidentally from Ken's mother, father, and older sister, was this: Ken had indeed climbed the tree and had indeed knocked the nest to the ground, killing the little birds. But Ken's mother was not angry and had *not* punished him. In fact, she had comforted the boy, who was weeping hysterically because he had "murdered" the birds, and had promised him a trip to the movies that Saturday.

When confronted with his family's memory of this event, Ken was astonished. After thinking about it, he admitted that he was unable to say which version was true.

This is, admittedly, a fairly dramatic illustration of memory distortion. Most psychiatrists would probably theorize that eight-year-old Ken felt so guilty about the accident that he felt he deserved punishment. Over time, he projected these internal guilt feelings onto an external image — that of his mother — and rein-vented the episode to include the punishment he felt was warranted.

It's unlikely that very many of our childhood memories are so completely changed by our unconscious needs or feelings. But it is possible that many of our childhood recollections may be colored or changed to some extent. For example, most adults, who have to bear substantial personal and work-related respon-sibility, tend to accept the traditional attitude that childhood is a happy and carefree period of life. Yet, given time for serious reflection, many of these same people would realize that, as children, they endured many difficult and unhappy periods.

Memory is not only changeable; it is also selective. We tend to remember what we consider the most significant events in our lives — whether they were happy or sad events — and not to remember the less special but far more numerous events that make up our everyday lives. Whereas we might remember what we did on our fourth birthday, how many of us can remember anything that happened on the day *after* our fourth birthday? What we tend to recall is a sort of condensed version of child-hood, a sense of peaks and valleys. Much of our childhood is simply lost to most of us.

It is important for a parent to realize that the fact that he was once a kid himself does not mean he will automatically under-stand or sympathize with every one of his own child's words, moods, and actions. Even if a parent did have complete and totally accurate memories of his own childhood, he would almost certainly encounter some difficulties in child rearing. The reason for this is simple: Any child is much more than a miniature version of her parents. She is very much an individual, with her own temperament and unique personal history. Her reaction to any event may well differ markedly from the reaction of her siblings, or her same-age friends.

Most parents begin to note evidence of a child's particular personality traits very early in the child's life. Indeed, in any group of infants, some will clearly appear to be more physically active than others. Some will seem more fussy or high-strung; others will fall naturally into regular eating and sleeping patterns. No one can fully explain the reasons why one newborn behaves differently from another, but some traits or tendencies do exist virtually at birth.

We mustn't exaggerate the importance of this, however. A child's emotional health and personality are certainly not pre-determined at birth. Rather, it is his environment — physical, intellectual, and emotional — that is overwhelmingly important in shaping personality. This is one more important reason why parents cannot expect magically to understand their sons and daughters simply by recalling their own childhood experiences. The fact is that our sons and daughters are growing up in a very different world from ours, and with very different parents: us.

To understand our own children, it helps to be familiar with the emotional and intellectual framework within which children act and grow. Just as there are observable landmarks in a child's physical development (first step, increase in coordination, growth spurt) so there are landmarks in the child's interior life. These invisible stages of a child's emotional and intellectual growth may cause him to behave in ways that puzzle or irritate even the most patient, loving parents. Certainly these stages will greatly affect the child's reaction to serious stress within the family, including the inevitable stress associated with parental separation and divorce.

Divorcing or separated parents will want to do everything possible to help their children through the difficult period of adjustment. This task will be easier if the parent understands, generally, how children of various ages come to understand themselves and others.

Consider a very common family scene: A baby sits contentedly in a playpen in the family dining room, playing with her simple toys. Her young mother and father are seated at the dining table, sipping their morning coffee, reading the newspaper, and exchanging occasional comments on their plans for the day ahead. In this scene, the play activities of the baby, on the one hand, and the relatively simple, ordinary actions of the parents, on the other, illustrate a developmental gap infinitely greater than the few feet between the playpen and dining table.

At first, these developmental differences between parent and child may seem so obvious and universal as to be beneath our consideration. But if we stop to give fresh thought to the differing capabilities of parent and child we discover them to be quite staggering.

The parents, for one thing, take it for granted that they have physically mastered their immediate environment. They can get themselves out of bed, and from bedroom to dining table. Not only do they possess the gross physical coordination and control necessary to stand, walk, and to climb stairs; they also assume the more finely tuned coordination required to dress themselves: to button shirts, pull zippers, tie shoes. Any adult who considers these feats ordinary should try to recall the very first time that he, as a child, succeeded in tying his own shoes. The sense of utter triumph and mastery this event engenders in a child is unmistakable.

Our playpen-bound baby knows nothing of this. Too young to walk or even crawl very far, her physical universe extends no farther than an arm's reach from whatever spot she's laid down in.

But the baby's intellectual and emotional development limits her even more than her physical capabilities. Her mother, casually reading a newspaper, is actually absorbing and processing a variety of highly sophisticated information and using abstract concepts (politics, law, economics) to put her own life into realistic perspective. She has learned enough of the world around her to see herself as a member of community, state, and country. She has verbal and intellectual skills that enable her to debate and discuss ideas, thus further establishing herself as a unique personality.

But even advanced physical and intellectual capabilities do not, without more, result in a mature, healthy adulthood. There are social skills — insight and sensitivity to the needs of others — acquired through years of interaction with family, lovers, and friends.

Both parents constantly draw on these social skills, either in leisure activities with friends or in business dealings with co-workers or clients. Both parents have gained a realistic sense of themselves as individuals and have learned to respect the thoughts and feelings of others. Finally, the young mother in our picture enjoys a mature, loving relationship with her husband, and he with her. Each spouse is, to the other, both caring and cared for. Each satisfies the other's need to love and to *be* loved. These parents demonstrate the realistic knowledge of self, as well as love and respect for others, that are the hallmark of emotional maturity.

The infant's limitations make hers a very different universe. She has none of the intellectual or emotional tools needed to evaluate realistically her own importance or the importance of others. On the contrary, the newborn is capable of knowing only her own immediate physical sensations. She can understand her needs of the moment — to be fed, or cleaned, or cared for — but nothing more. The baby's feelings are a direct result of physical sensations.

Thus, the infant may feel anger or helplessness at being hungry or soiled. But she can draw no generalized or abstract conclusions from these feelings. No infant is capable of generalizing from the immediate realization that "I'm hungry" to the reasonable consideration of "Well, Mother does feed me regularly, after all. I'm sure she won't let me starve. I'll just lie here quietly until dinner time." Rather, as any adult veteran of the two o'clock feeding can testify, the infant is aware only of an uncomfortable sensation (hunger). This is an immediate need followed by an immediate protest — crying. A baby simply cannot imagine the future; she cannot put things off. Only the present exists for her; she must be fed *now*.

Obviously, as a child grows older, he develops much more sophisticated skills and a more mature view of his world. The more a child's behavior mimics an adult's — the more mature he *appears* to be — the more his parents are apt to assume that his reactions to important events should be identical to theirs. This is a common, but potentially a very troublesome, misconception among parents.

It is absolutely essential for the parent to realize that, until the child reaches young adulthood, his view of the world and the people around him is very different from the adult's. Even the teen-ager, who appears full-grown in so many ways, is somewhat at the mercy of his continuing physical and emotional development. Your behavior toward your child, whatever his age, during the period of parental separation and divorce must take into account his particular stage of development.

What's more, the nature and quality of your child's personal growth will depend largely on you. No child grows in a vacuum; he learns by doing, by acting, by *interacting* with other people.

You, the parent, are a most important person in your child's life; you will play a unique and vital role in his development. Even your newborn is learning to respond to other people through experiencing your responses to him. Your relationship with your child will have enormous implications for his future. It is the way parents and their children behave *together* that teaches the child how to experience his world.

Though we commonly refer to child development as consisting of stages, as if children actually hop up from one precise level of performance to another, the child's growth is of course more gradual and subtle. Also, there are individual variations among children, so that no one child may fit exactly into his theoretical stage at a given time. However, there are certain significant events in a child's overall emotional growth that parents will want to expect and understand.

At birth, as we have said, the infant has very little idea that a world exists that is apart from and independent of his own needs. Rather, he believes that he himself is the entire universe. Nothing exists, in the infant's perception, except to care for his own feelings and needs.

At some point around the ages of six to eight months, the infant will first come to notice the independent existence of the person who generally cares for his physical needs by feeding, cleaning, and cuddling him. This caretaker becomes the first other person in the infant's life; until now he had not understood that his food, dry diapers, and soothing lullabies did not magically emerge out of thin air.

The caretaker is usually, but not necessarily, the infant's mother. Of course it could be, in some cases, the baby's father, or a housekeeper or nurse, or any other person who has the primary responsibility for the baby's day-to-day physical care.

How an infant successfully recognizes one adult above all others is not fully understood, but there is some intriguing evidence suggesting that the six-month-old's perceptions may be quite sophisticated in this respect. Some experts who have studied children of this age hold that the infant is capable of distinguishing its mother from all other persons, including the adult who is its primary caretaker. Thus, an infant whose mother works full-time and who is cared for every day by a live-in nurse, may still recognize its mother as a particularly special and unique person. This notion of a special mother-infant recognition factor may well be true, though it may be difficult to establish as a scientific fact. Researchers are only beginning to explore the full implications of mother-infant bonding, and it appears quite possible that certain events occurring during a mother's pregnancy and immediately after her baby's birth may greatly affect the mother-infant relationship. There are also exciting implications in this research for the possibilities of father-infant bonding, an area that until now has not been satisfactorily explored.

At this stage of six or eight months, then, the infant first understands that she is not the only human being in the universe, that there exists another individual who cares for her needs. Moreover, she quickly learns to distinguish this special person from all others. One very common result of this newfound ability to single out the caretaker is something we call "stranger anxiety." Parents often notice that their six-month-old child begins, for the first time, to cry or exhibit other signs of fear or discomfort when in the presence of unfamiliar persons. Many an adoring grandparent, tired after a long trip made especially to greet the new grandchild, has been offended when his or her affectionate hugs drew immediate howls of fear and protest from the infant.

Stranger anxiety, however embarrassing to the proud parent, is actually a sign of healthy emotional development. It indicates that the infant, having learned to recognize the good, caretaking adult, has also learned to take note of unfamiliar faces. At this stage, the baby is puzzled and frightened by unfamiliar faces; they have no place in her tiny universe.

The parent is, naturally, touched and heartened by the baby's obvious recognition of and responsiveness to her. The infantile cooing and gurgling noises, and the excited flailing of tiny arms and feet on seeing or being touched by the parent, clearly indicate that the child has established a special relationship with the parent.

But the child, at this early age, is not yet capable of appreciating that a parent, or any other person, has her own thoughts, needs, and feelings — her own personality. Rather, the infant still believes that he, and he alone, is the center of the world. Other people exist only to the extent that they affect the infant himself.

Psychiatrists and others who work with children have a word for the young child's preoccupation with himself and his own needs. They call it "egocentricity." Egocentricity is entirely normal and healthy in small children; they are not capable of thinking in any other way. Indeed, as we shall see, a marked degree of egocentricity continues well through childhood and into adolescence. It is the central mark of adulthood that a person has fully learned to appreciate and consider the needs and feelings of others.

But all of us, even as adults, remain egocentric to some degree. That is, we all continue to consider our own interest as an important motive for action throughout our lives. Such questions as "What sort of education is best for me? What type of work will I be doing?" and even, "What sort of man (or woman) will meet my emotional needs as a spouse?" all involve perfectly rational, egocentric considerations. In the rational, mature adult, egocentricity is synonymous with enlightened self-interest. It is very different from the child's limited, self-centered view of the world.

But in times of crisis or stress, such as a divorce, egocentricity tends to become pronounced or distorted in even the healthiest, most stable adult. Confused, frightened, angry, we feel the egocentric child in all of us straining to take control. Even at this difficult time the loving parent, with his superior understanding, must try to subject his own feelings and immediate self-interest to the best interests of his child.

To say that children are largely egocentric in their thinking does not imply that they are incapable of truly loving their parents, or feeling affection for others close to them. The child who throws his arms around his parent, exclaiming "I love you," is expressing very real warmth and affection. In fact, love feelings in a child are usually very intense, so intense that children will commonly make excuses for a parent's obvious flaws, or boast of his exaggerated importance or abilities.

Parents are often disappointed when, during times of tension and upset, children do not behave as adults. But such expectations are unrealistic. As the child's intellectual, emotional, and physical sophistication increases, he will gradually learn that other people are worthy of the same attention, affection, and respect that he expects to enjoy. Because of his natural preoccupation with himself and his own needs, the growing child makes certain unrealistic suppositions about his own importance in the world. He simply cannot imagine that any event can happen without some relation to himself. Instead, the young child imagines that, in some way, everything that happens occurs *because* of him. He feels that he is responsible, to some extent, for literally everything. Such thinking in children is called "magical thinking." Magical thinking is most dominant in children in the ages from two to six years, but remnants of it may continue throughout childhood.

Magical thinking is a result, in a sense, of the child's perception that he is all-powerful, that he causes all things to happen. Such thinking can lead not only to feelings of omnipotence, but to guilt and distress on the child's part. An understanding of magical thinking will help you to comprehend your child's sometimes puzzling reactions to your divorce.

One example of magical thinking, and the anguish it can cause in a child, is seen in the case of a five-year-old named Nan. Nan was — and is — a normal child in all respects: bright, healthy, and loving. For a period of several months following her fifth birthday, Nan's parents took her along, at least once a week, to visit the home of her ailing maternal grandfather. The grandfather was by then quite elderly, and terminally ill, and in no condition to play with or respond to a child. Nan, in turn, was terrified of her grandfather, of what she perceived to be his gruff manner, and of the oxygen tanks and other strange medical equipment that surrounded him. She would cry before each visit and beg her parents not to make her go along. Nan was afraid to tell her parents that she didn't like her grandfather; she sensed that was a bad way to feel. The parents, understandably, did not guess the true nature of Nan's feelings, and thought that her crying scenes were just temper tantrums.

Eventually, after a lengthy illness, Nan's grandfather died. Though she said little to her parents about the death, and appeared at first to be unaffected, it soon became apparent that Nan was overwhelmed with feelings of anxiety and guilt. She was convinced that her all-powerful feelings of fear and distrust of her grandfather and her desire to be free of visiting him had literally killed him. Her bad thoughts, the girl felt, had made her a murderer. Nan needed the tactful yet persistent reassurance of her parents before she could understand that she was not responsible for the elderly man's death.

As Nan's case illustrates, children, because they engage in magical thinking, cannot understand the difference between thought an action. Nan was convinced that her thoughts could kill. Her egocentric view of life made her feel, in a way, all-powerful. Similarly, all children of Nan's age think that their wishes or desires can determine the actions of other people. The child at this age feels like an omnipotent being: She simply cannot yet comprehend the adult concept of cause and effect.

Magical thinking is a normal and healthy aspect of the child's development. It will persist, to some degree, until early adolescence. At the age of twelve or thirteen, the child will begin to think in more abstract, less me-oriented terms.

But magical thinking may become a problem for children when, for any reason, it makes them feel guilty or bad. It is important to understand that even very young children are capable of experiencing guilt. Some psychologists and child development experts, in fact, hold that a child as young as three months can be made to feel guilty. Whether or not one accepts that theory, it seems clear that a child by age one, and certainly by age two, can be made to feel guilty or ashamed of his behavior. We have all seen, for example, the guilty or embarrassed expression on the face of an eighteen-month-old child who has accidentally broken something and been reprimanded by his parents.

It is vital to appreciate the strength of the child's magical view of the world, and the child's sense of guilt, in order to help him through the difficult period of separation and divorce. Otherwise the child, who is often too young to comprehend fully his parents' real reasons for divorce, may suffer profound and unnecessary anguish or even permanent psychological harm.

Consider Robert, an appealing seven-year-old who ultimately had to have professional help after his parents' divorce. Before his mother left Robert, his father, and his two brothers, Robert had had regular arguments with her over his reluctance to help with household chores. As most parents can attest, Robert's behavior was entirely normal for a child of his age. Robert, however, was too young to appreciate the full implications of the continuing tension between his father and mother, and the heated arguments between them over his mother's drinking problem.

After several months of these arguments, Robert's mother suddenly, and without telling her children, left her family and moved to another town. Confused and saddened, Robert drew an obvious magical conclusion to explain her departure: He was convinced that he had forced his mother to leave because "I wouldn't pick up my room." Robert's magical thinking in this case resulted in deep-seated guilt feelings, which finally required the help of a psychotherapist.

Some mental-health professionals hold that magical thinking makes a child particularly vulnerable during certain specific stages of his development. Most of these experts would point to the so-called oedipal phase as a particularly significant time in the child's life.

It is important to realize that the whole issue of the Oedipus complex has become a controversial one, and that the concept itself has been interpreted in different ways. Still, the idea is an important one in psychiatry, and one that may have special relevance to the children of divorce. There follows, then, what I hope is a fair, if simplified, exploration of the oedipal theory.

Traditional psychoanalytic theory holds that a child, particularly a little boy, experiences his oedipal phase between the ages of about three and five. The word *oedipal*, of course, comes from the ancient Greek story of Oedipus, who, meeting his own mother after many years' separation, and unaware of their relationship, fell in love with her.

When psychiatrists and others today speak of the oedipal phase, they mean that, around the age of three, the child becomes aware of his own sexual feelings. In a general way, he also becomes aware of the differences between the sexes. This does not mean that a three-year-old is an expert on human anatomy; it simply means that, by that time, he has a definite perception that men are somehow different from women.

The oedipal theory states that the three- to five-year-old boy focuses his sexual feelings on his mother, who, after all, is quite possibly the most important person, and certainly the most important female, in his life. The little boy desires to possess his mother in some exclusive way (the little girl, of course, would theoretically focus similar feelings on her father). He becomes jealous of others whom he sees as competitors for his mother's love and attention.

In order completely to possess his opposite-sex parent, the child may begin to wish that the same-sex parent would somehow go away. He invents, in his own mind, a sort of rivalry with the same-sex parent. But the child is not comfortable with his imagined rivalry. He begins to fear the anger of his rival, who is after all much larger and more powerful than the child. He may imagine that his same-sex parent will use his superior size and strength to punish him for his bad thoughts. These thoughts, naturally, make the child very anxious. The anxiety that the intense attachment to the opposite-sex parent and fear of the same-sex parent create is called the Oedipus conflict.

Obviously, the child does not carry these uncomfortable feelings all through life. How, then, is the Oedipus conflict resolved? Psychoanalytic theory holds that the child learns to defend himself against fear of his powerful grown-up rival by a process known as identification. That is, he attempts to imitate the potentially threatening same-sex parent, to take on that parent's characteristics, in order to make himself feel as powerful as the grownup. The child (again, this applies most obviously to boys) then eventually abandons the idea of completely possessing the opposite-sex parent and decides, instead, to imitate his father and search for someone like his mother. In other words, the little boy, by age four or five, decides that "I want a girl just like the girl that married dear old Dad."

The whole concept of the Oedipus conflict is widely misunderstood and causes undue anxiety in some parents. One reason for this anxiety is that many parents are uncomfortable with the notion that such small children have sexual feelings at all, let alone sexual feelings that relate to the parent. But the fact is that all children, including newborns, do experience sexual sensations of some kind.

It is easy, however, for a parent to misinterpret the sort of sexual feelings that a child experiences during the oedipal phase. The oedipal theory does not necessarily mean, as some believe, that the child actually wants to have sexual intercourse with the opposite-sex parent. Indeed, most children at this early age have no clear idea of exactly what sexual intercourse is. Rather, sexual feelings, in this context, may be more generalized warm feelings, part of the child's desire to have the loved parent "all to myself." Such feelings are common to all children and a vital part of normal development. They are part of a child's first experience of having a loving, one-to-one relationship with another person. Parents have no reason to be afraid of or embarrassed by their child's sexuality; they should react instead with rationality and understanding.

Often, the child's same-sex parent must call on an extra measure of patience during this period, for the oedipal child can be exasperating, in small ways. This is the period, for example, when the child may decide that the favored opposite-sex parent, now an object of special love, does all things perfectly, while the same-sex parent does everything wrong. The little girl may insist that only her father dress and bathe her and may complain or cry when her mother must do it. The little boy of this age may behave in exactly the same fashion, only in his case Mother will be his favored and constant companion.

The child's apparent indifference to — or even occasional hostility toward — his same-sex parent can be very hurtful to that parent, if he does not understand the child's underlying emotional struggle. The little boy who appears not to appreciate anything that his father does for him, but who constantly displays his love and affection toward his mother, sends out signals that can easily be misread. The same-sex parent may begin to feel disappointment, rejection, even jealousy over his child's unfair behavior.

Fortunately for everyone, in this case the old cliché is true: The oedipal phase is just a stage. While it continues, the same-sex parent must realize that the child's behavior toward the parent does not really reflect a lack of affection. Rather, the child is learning to come to grips with a new and complex set of emotions.

Why is this discussion of the oedipal phase relevant to a family whose parents are separating or divorcing? Because some psychiatrists hold that a child whose parents separate or divorce during his oedipal phase is especially vulnerable to psychological harm. This may not be universally true; still, a parent should be very much aware of the thoughts and feelings a child of this age might be experiencing.

A child in the oedipal phase — three to five years old — is also at the age where egocentricity and magical thinking are common. The combination of these elements can lead to problems for some children. Four-year-old Kenneth, for example, had the normal oedipal wishes and fantasies of possession of his mother and rivalry with his father. His parents' marriage had been unstable for some time, and finally Kenneth's father moved out of the house to live with another woman. Kenneth then became convinced that he had forced his father out of the house and had won sole possession, as it were, of his mother. He had triumphed, in his mind, over his father-rival.

But such a victory over a parent-rival is actually very damaging to a child, for this is a battle that the child, in his heart, does not want to win. Kenneth soon began to exhibit signs of anxiety, including bed-wetting and frequent, violent, temper tantrums. He was, in fact, experiencing severe guilt at the thought of having won his mother away from his father.

So, a child in the oedipal phase may be more likely to feel

responsible for his parents' separation and divorce, for he imagines himself to be part of a love triangle that caused his parents' marriage to end. There are ways, which we will later discuss, by which a parent can help a child to understand that divorce is not the child's fault. It is worth mentioning here briefly, however, that a parent can unwittingly *increase* a child's feeling of responsibility for divorce by treating him in ways inappropriate for his young age.

A newly divorced mother, for example, may innocently tell her young son that he is now "the man of the house" or that he must in other ways behave as though he were an adult. In this and other ways boys or girls may come to believe that they must act the role of surrogate spouse to their now-single parent. It is understandable that a newly separated parent may want to rely emotionally on his or her children, but such a parent can easily lose sight of the fact that children cannot understand or cope with the demand that they behave in ways inappropriate to their years and experience. As we shall see, this kind of extraordinary pressure can be harmful to a child of any age.

Magical thinking and egocentricity are no doubt strongest in young children, but what about older children and adolescents? Their attitudes are not very different in basic outline from that of their younger brothers and sisters. Though of course they are much more sophisticated, these older children remain egocentric to some extent. They, too, are apt to misunderstand or misinterpret their true role in their parents' divorce.

From ages six to twelve, the child is in what psychoanalysts call the latency period. This term refers to the fact that a child's sexual feelings are thought by some to be latent at this point in his development. This is another psychoanalytic notion that is somewhat controversial, and newer studies seem to indicate that a child's sexual impulses are not truly latent at this or any other time in his life. But the *latency period* is a widely accepted phase, and it will be used here to refer to the six- to twelve-year-old child.

A child in the latency period is still not really capable of the sophisticated abstract thinking necessary to view her world objectively. She still tends to exaggerate her own role in the scheme of things and to feel that her actions and thoughts can have a disproportionate effect on events. A child of this age is certainly not so completely egocentric as an infant or toddler, but she is markedly more ego-centered than the mature adult.

Adolescents, though their thinking is much more sophisticated, are egocentric for another reason. Though they may be intellectually quite advanced, adolescents are trying to define themselves, to discover their own unique style, talents, and goals. They can do this most easily by comparing themselves with the adults they know. Thus, adolescent rebellion, which occurs in each generation of teen-agers, is really a form of comparison: The adolescent is rebelling against his closest models, his parents. The adolescent girl or boy must test out different ways of thinking, dressing, and acting, before discovering what will become a comfortable personal style. Since the teen-aged child can seem so stubborn and fiercely independent, it is sometimes hard for his parents to realize how much he needs and relies on them.

But for even the rebellious teen-ager, parents represent stability and permanence. After all, a teen-ager often feels that he can safely rebel with new behavior largely because, after the experiment, he will come home to his parents, his emotional Rock of Gibraltar. Divorce, which represents a loss of permanence and stability, can be extremely threatening to the adolescent. Indeed, some experts feel that the teen-aged child is even more likely to experience psychological damage due to divorce than is the young child in the oedipal period.

The teen-ager's particular brand of egocentricity may lead him to react to divorce in ways that parents find hard to understand. Tommy, a previously quiet, well-mannered fifteen-year-old, reacted to his parents' separation and divorce by "acting out" his feelings of anger and fear. Tommy's reaction took the form of aggressive, violent behavior, including schoolyard fistfights and episodes of vandalism. He began to seek out a new type of friend, eventually becoming part of a small group of "tough" habitual truants. All this, coupled with increasingly frequent bouts of alcohol abuse, eventually necessitated the intervention of a psychiatrist. Tommy, it developed, saw his parents' divorce as literally the disintegration of his world. His violent behavior was a desperate lashing out, triggered by his anger and despair.

A much more common, but puzzling, teen-age reaction to divorce takes the form of no apparent reaction at all. A typical example of this behavior was shown by Gwen, aged fourteen, who appeared totally unconcerned when told of her parents' impending divorce. But from that time on, Gwen seemed to be less and less involved with her family. Instead, she threw herself into her high school activities and often stayed on after class to talk to one or another favorite teacher. Her friends seemed to become more important to her, and she spent endless hours visiting them or talking with them on the phone. To her parents, who were very upset over the breaking up of the family unit, Gwen's behavior was both puzzling and hurtful. It was, as Gwen's mother put it, "like a slap in the face. We thought she just didn't care about us anymore."

But Gwen did care about her family. What she was actually doing was protecting herself, by putting emotional distance between herself and the divorce. Threatened by the loss of a major emotional anchor, her parents' marriage, Gwen reached out to other people for support. At that difficult time, she needed the companionship and sense of belonging she felt when she was with her friends. She also needed the new adult role models she saw in her teachers. Gwen's reaction was self-protective, although disturbing to her parents, who had actually hoped to rely on her for emotional support. But Gwen was reacting in a normal and healthy way: Her interests outside the home helped her to weather her parents' divorce.

Egocentricity, then, is a powerful intellectual component in children, throughout childhood and adolescence. It will certainly influence your child's perceptions during divorce or separation. We have already seen one very common way in which this happens, when the small child blames himself for the divorce. Some of the more serious effects of this thinking in a child — such as depression, "acting out," or other self-destructive behavior — will be examined in detail later.

We should note, however, one other very important, and very common, result of the child's egocentric mind-set: reconciliation fantasies, which occur when the child feels responsible for "making everything O.K.," for bringing separated parents back together. This sense of responsibility, with all the guilt and frustration it can bring, has been observed in children as young as two.

Almost inevitably, the child who sees her parents separating will feel threatened, to some extent, by this major change in her life and will wish her parents to reconcile. (Of course, if the marriage has been so troubled as to be absolutely frightening to the child — for example, where the parents have been physically violent — the child may actually be relieved to see it end.) Since the child greatly exaggerates the influence of her own thoughts and feelings on others, she may well feel that she can literally "wish" the parents back together. And she will feel guilty and frustrated when her magical wishes do not succeed.

A child may not always express these reconciliation fantasies directly, but she may secretly act on them. She may, for example, go to great lengths to force her separated parents to meet and deal with each other, in the hope that they will make up. In fact, children often turn themselves into problem children in hope of bringing their parents back together.

Ten-year-old Ellen had always gotten straight A's in school before her parents' separation. She loved school, and was a voracious reader with a lively curiosity. After the separation, however, Ellen started to have problems with her schoolwork. By the end of the first term after her parents' separation she had actually failed in several of her school subjects. Neither Ellen's teacher nor her parents could discern any reason for this, except to say that the child was "upset."

In fact, Ellen was deliberately failing in school, because her failure encouraged contact between her separated mother and father. Ordinarily, the parents rarely spoke to or saw each other. But when Ellen's performance at school changed so drastically, her worried parents naturally felt obligated to get together to discuss the girl's problems. Ellen was using her school failures to fan her hopes that she could encourage her parents so see each other more frequently — and eventually to reconcile.

Reconciliation fantasies can persist in children long after parents actually divorce. Later, we will examine some ways in which parents can help their children give up these groundless hopes.

Parents should be aware of one other basic aspect of their child's intellect that will affect his immediate reaction to parental divorce. This is the child's sense of the concrete.

A small child is simply unable to engage in sophisticated abstract thinking. Because of this, his reaction to news of his parents' divorce may take the form of a preoccupation with very concrete problems. He may want to know, for example, "Will I still have my own bedroom?" or "Will Daddy still take me to the zoo?"

Parents often react with disappointment to questions like this, thinking that they reflect their child's selfishness or inability to comprehend that an important change is taking place in the family's life. Parents must understand, however, that the young child's understanding is often limited to these very real concerns.

Similarly, the older child, who *can* think in more global terms, is often so threatened by the wider implications of the divorce that he fastens on small concrete problems over which he feels he has some control. If the child can assure himself that such important and basic questions as "Where will I live?" and "Will you still come to my birthday party?" have been satisfactorily answered, he may comfort himself that his familiar world will not disintegrate entirely after the divorce.

In short, what may initially seem a selfish reaction on the child's part is usually the child's attempt to convince himself that he has some control over a course of events that will radically change his life and that he finds very frightening. An understanding parent can do much to help his child over these fears.

2

Explaining Divorce to Your Child

AS EVERY PARENT KNOWS, the young child's favorite question is "Why?" Your children will have hundreds of "whys?" about your separation or divorce, whether or not they verbalize them at first. In this situation, you should be alert for and encourage the "whys?" They are a sign that your child is trying to understand and come to grips with a very upsetting event.

Parents frequently tell me they believe that to explain too much about the end of their marriage to their children will unduly upset or confuse the children. Indeed, some parents even think that smaller children should be told nothing at all.

But I believe that parents who shy away from telling their children about the divorce are trying to protect themselves, not the children. Nearly every parent involved in a divorce has some feelings of guilt or shame over the failure of the marriage. Even though society looks at divorce with more tolerance than it did formerly, there is still a certain amount of social as well as personal embarrassment surrounding any divorce. And, inevitably, the divorcing parent is experiencing other negative feelings: anger, grief, and frustration.

Under the circumstances, you may understandably feel that discussing the divorce with your child may become a most unpleasant rehashing of the whole experience. You may also fear that your child will become hysterical, or grief-stricken, or blame you and come to hate you. Finally, you may well fear that sitting down to discuss this painful subject with your child may cause you to lose your own emotional self-control.

But it is essential that you overcome your fears and resolve to discuss the entire process of the separation and divorce with your children, including very young children. Of course, the discussion must be designed for the child's age and understanding. But a child who is old enough to notice that Daddy is no longer around the house or that Mommy is crying all the time is entitled to an explanation of where Daddy's gone or why Mommy's sad.

Why is it so important that the child be told? Children have an uncanny ability to know when they're being lied to. Statements that are patently false (a crying mother saying that she's "O.K.") or evasive ("Daddy's just away on business") can cause a child serious distress. For one thing, they deprive the child of the only handle — the truth — he may use to try to gain some degree of control over a difficult situation. The child who knows that Daddy is *not* just away on business, but does not know where Daddy is, may become extremely anxious. After all, one of his parents has disappeared, or may return to visit only sporadically, and the child feels that he has no control over these mysterious circumstances. If the child knew the truth in some detail (that Daddy had gone to live in a new house on Maple Street, for example, and that he would come to visit every Saturday) he would feel more the master of the situation and be less frightened by it.

Similarly, it can be very damaging to a child to know that a parent is lying to her. A four-year-old or even a two-year-old clearly *knows* that her weeping mother is not "O.K." And the five-year-old who's been told that "Mommy will be back soon" will definitely feel she's been lied to when Mommy simply doesn't return. Children whose parents lie to them not only experience resentment but may also feel anxiety or even panic. Remember, most children feel that their parents are the most important and powerful people in the world. When the child realizes that these most important people are not to be trusted, she may well feel that her universe is collapsing. The child who can no longer trust her parents to be honest with her may understandably feel that she has nowhere left to turn. To a small child, particularly, these feelings can be devastating.

To some extent, parents who do not want to talk about their divorce with their children may also be genuinely concerned with protecting the children against unnecessary stress. They have heard that children of divorced parents are in greater danger of experiencing psychological difficulties than are children of "intact" homes. They fear for their children, and try, in their way, to protect the children from these disturbing events.

It may be advisable here to confront the question of psychological risk for the child of divorce. It is statistically true, in fact, that children of divorce are somewhat more likely than other children to experience some sort of psychological problems, though not all children with problems will need professional care. But, as usual, statistics do not tell the whole story. Before getting carried away by guilt, divorcing parents should look at the broader picture.

Most parents believe that divorce causes problems in children simply because it means, in most instances, that the child will be raised primarily by only one natural parent. In effect, the common wisdom has it, such a child will be injured by being brought up by "only" a natural mother, or "only" a natural father. But the available evidence does not support this proposition.

What it does show, to my mind, is that children of divorce who suffer from psychological troubles do so because they have been exposed to *excessive conflict* between their parents. Parents can do much to minimize the painful conflict to which children are often subject during and after their parents' divorce.

Let's look at one interesting fact. The evidence available to us suggests that children who have experienced the death of one parent are, like children of divorce, at slightly higher risk psychologically. But the evidence also indicates that these bereaved children are at *less* risk than the children of divorce. This would seem to indicate that there are factors other than the physical loss of a parent or being raised in a single-parent home at work here. The answer lies in the fact that the bereaved child, though he experiences profound grief, has not ordinarily been subject to the stress of prolonged conflict between his parents.

Similarly, some of the unhappiest children I have seen have come from intact but strife-filled homes. As we will discuss more fully later, there are couples who stay together because of a need to engage each other in unhealthy and self-destructive games. The result is often incessant violent argument or sadistic bickering. Often the child is dragged into the struggle, sometimes becoming the unhappy pawn of his parents. Ten-year-old Daniel spent most of his mealtimes hearing himself the subject of his parents' arguments. The mother and father claimed to have very different thoughts on the subject of child rearing, so poor Daniel was trapped: If he acted to please one, he offended the other. In fact, Daniel's parents' child-rearing theories were merely an excuse for them to argue; had they been childless, they would have found another excuse. Daniel could not know this and eventually became so depressed that his parents were forced to seek professional help for him.

Of course, there are also profoundly unhappy couples who

stay together out of the deep religious convictions of one or both parents. Children of these couples often live in an atmosphere of constant tension, acutely aware that no real love exists between their parents.

It would seem, then, that while the physical loss of a parent through death or separation may make a child psychologically vulnerable, constant parental conflict is potentially much more likely to damage the child. This discovery has two very important implications. First, it points to the fact that unhappy parents who "stay together for the sake of the children" are probably making a mistake. The second, and more hopeful, implication is that parents who work at minimizing conflict during divorce can greatly help their children to a healthy adjustment to the situation.

A generation ago, countless couples, out of religious conviction or concern for the children, put up with loveless, unhappy marriages till their children were grown. Even today, I frequently hear of couples who mutually promise to endure each other as partners in order to spare their children the pain or trauma of divorce.

Unfortunately, if one talks to the now-grown children of some of these loveless marriages, one sometimes hears real horror stories of childhoods lived in anxiety, guilt, and fear. One such child, a successful professional man, admits that it would have been better for him if his parents had ended the charade. "They rarely talked to each other," he says now. "The tension was constant, and unbearable. It was clear that they wanted nothing to do with each other."

Children are very sensitive to levels of feeling between their parents: Constant fighting, cold hatred, or even a basic lack of interest between parents are felt by children and contribute to feelings of insecurity that may cause psychological damage. It is very difficult for me to believe that children can benefit from parents who remain together only for the children's sake. I think it's time that parents put this particular burden of guilt aside and decide that there are better reasons for them to preserve — or end — their marriage.

What *is* important is to try your best to minimize strife during the period of separation and divorce. This does not mean that you must hide your very real negative feelings at this time. It means, as we shall see later, that there are ways of dealing with these feelings that can reduce the child's own doubts and fears. This requires, to be sure, that you sometimes put your own immediate needs after those of your children. I know how difficult this can be, especially at such an unhappy and anxious time. But, if you can come to understand and respond to your children's needs at this time, it will almost certainly aid them in coming to a realistic and healthy acceptance of the divorce.

Children then, including the very young, ought to be told some of the particulars about the separation and divorce of their parents. Before going into the details of how this ought to be done, I feel obliged to state what I'm sure is an obvious truth: That is, not all children are the same. Not all children will react to such news in the same way.

I have discussed, to some extent, the way in which the child's perceptions change as he grows older. But children do not differ only in age; they differ, too, in temperament. Any parent looking at the personality differences between his children can attest to this. These personality traits that distinguish the child as an individual develop and grow with the child. They account for what may be very different reactions among children in the same family to news of their parents' divorce. I have no doubt that certain children are more psychologically resilient than others, although psychiatrists do not know all the reasons for this. In any event, it is important to be aware that children in the same family may react very differently in times of stress. One little boy may appear to miss his absent father greatly, while his brother may display no such feelings. These different reactions do not necessarily mean that one child is normal and the other sick: They are merely expressions of individual temperament.

What is the appropriate time to tell your children of your impending separation or divorce? There is never going to be a perfect moment. But with a little thought and planning, you can take certain precautions that will ultimately make the news easier for your child to understand and accept.

The first is that the children should not be told until the decision to divorce or separate is *definitely* made. You want to avoid "crying wolf," that is, staging a painful and dramatic scene about divorce if there is still a real chance of reconciliation. One marriage partner may be tempted to do this just to show the spouse that she means business, that he better shape up or ship out. But it is obviously damaging to hit a child with news of a divorce, then compound his understandable upset with later confusion when the divorce doesn't occur. Parents who create such scenes and use divorce as a frequent but empty threat can do their children great harm. The children will not only come to feel that they are being lied to, they will also have to face constant uncertainty, which will make them feel that their world is in perpetual jeopardy.

Neither should you wait until the last minute, long after the final decision is made, to inform the child. The child's emotional world does not comprehend the detached legal proceedings of the divorce court. He does not necessarily know — or care — that "the action has yet to be filed" or that "the divorce decree has been finalized." To a child, the significant event is the fact that Daddy and Mommy will no longer be together. When that decision has been made, the emotional climate in the child's home changes, and the child has a right to be told.

Ideally, parents should sit down *together* with the children to tell them of the divorce. Obviously this is impossible in cases where one spouse has physically abandoned the family. And I do recognize that it is a difficult thing, in many cases, for parents who are extremely angry or upset with each other to sit down and discuss these painful details. But I firmly believe that it is the responsibility of both parents to do so.

Why is this so important? For one thing, so that the child will see that, even in the divorce situation, the parents can deal reasonably with each other. This does not mean that you must act perfectly calm and detached. On the contrary, such detachment may only confuse the child, who will then not understand why the marriage is ending. It is important, however, that the child understand that both Mommy and Daddy are involved in the decision to divorce.

Another, related, consideration has to do with the child's fears and fantasies. If Mommy alone, or Daddy alone, tells the child of the divorce, the child will begin to wonder about the role of the other parent. He may imagine that something terrible has happened to the other parent. Most important, he may refuse to accept or believe the news about the divorce. Such was the case with six-year-old Molly. Molly's mother told her about the impending divorce several days after Molly's father had already moved out of the house. Molly reacted by simply refusing to believe her. She was overheard telling her friends that "Mommy says she wants a divorce, but Daddy doesn't. He'll be back."

Molly, in this case, was using a mechanism called denial to protect herself against the painful news of her parents' divorce. We shall say more about denial later. But it is important to note here that Molly was able to deny the truth in part because her father had never personally told her of *his* decision to divorce. Children of all ages are more likely to see the realities of the divorce situation if both parents tell them the news.

Some parents feel that, when there is more than one child in a family, the children should be told separately. Parents tend to feel this way particularly when the age range of the children is great. As one parent put it, "My four-year-old can't understand as much as my thirteen-year-old. Besides, each child deserves special attention. I'm cheating them if I try to tell them together."

I believe that this is a mistake. Just as parents should sit down together with their children at this time, it is important that the entire family unit should experience this occasion together. For one thing, telling the children separately can lead to resentment and confusion. "What's the big mystery?" the child may think. "What's my brother being told that I'm not being told?" Older children may feel that, in being singled out, they are having an unwanted responsibility placed on them to act as adults. Younger children may feel, on the other hand, that they are being treated like babies.

Second, and perhaps more important, this is an occasion that, if shared, can enable siblings to be of great support to one another. It can help to bind the children together in the difficult period of parental separation that they now face. It has been shown that many children who lose the physical presence of a parent — by either death or divorce — begin to parent each other. In some instances, they become especially close and are particularly attentive to each other's needs.

This can be true of children as young as four or five. As one young woman recalled her parents' divorce, "Dad was gone, and Mom was upset a lot — too upset to pay much attention to us. I was only five. If it hadn't been for my eight-year-old brother, I would have been lost. He kind of fathered me, I guess. And even though I was younger, I kind of took care of him, too — listening to his problems, cheering him up. I remember, he even used to tell me bedtime stories."

This kind of closeness among siblings should certainly be encouraged, and telling your children about the divorce all at once can help them understand that "we're all in this thing together."

No matter what the reasons for or circumstances of the divorce, there are two things about which the child must be constantly reassured. The first is that, while Mommy and Daddy may not now love each other, they still *do* love the child. This is vitally important. A child who sees that the grownups in his life no longer care for each other is naturally going to wonder how he himself will fare in this new situation. The parent who retains custody of the child must reassure him that he will be taken care of, as he has always been. And the noncustodial parent must also find ways to express his continuing love and interest in the child.

The second thing your child must be made to understand is that the divorce *is not his fault.* We have seen how the child's egocentricity colors his thinking. Often egocentricity will lead a child to hold himself responsible, in some way, for the divorce. It is important to know that the child may think this even though he never says anything about it. In fact, the child who blames himself for the divorce will often be afraid to verbalize his feelings. Therefore, parents should take the initiative. *Both* parents should reassure the child that his thoughts and actions had nothing to do with his parents' decision to end their marriage.

Many parents wonder whether their children should be told the real reasons for the divorce. In particularly painful situations, such as those involving alcoholism or marital infidelity, they may fear that such news would harm the child. But children have a right to know the truth. Even problems like alcoholism, if properly explained, can be understood by young children. Knowing the real reasons for the divorce will help the child to accept the finality of the decision and help to allay reconciliation fantasies.

Also, there is the danger that children who are not told the truth will learn it anyway, from another source. Nine-year-old

Marilyn's mother had told her only that Daddy had "gone away" and "wouldn't be living here anymore." Marilyn had long been aware of the constant fighting between her parents, but was afraid to ask her mother for more information. Marilyn finally found out the truth the hard way, when, at a family birthday party, a young cousin informed her that her father was a compulsive gambler, who had lost his job along with the family savings. Marilyn, needless to say, was shocked and confused by this news.

In cases like this, which are all too common, the child suffers for two reasons. Marilyn not only had to deal with the fact that her parents had been dishonest with her. She also was told of her father's problems in the least sympathetic light: He was a gambler, a "bad" person. How much better it would have been for her if her parents — or one of them — had been able to tell her that her father suffered from a kind of illness, compulsive gambling, over which he had no control. If Marilyn had been made to see that her father had a gambling problem, rather than innate bad character, she would have been much better able to cope with the inevitable comments and taunts of other children.

Children will be much more likely to accept and come to terms with the divorce if they know the true reasons for it. But it is not necessary to tell your children embarrassing or inappropriate details. For example, parents should not discuss the quality of their sex life together with their children. I know some parents consider this sort of extreme openness to be enlightened, but the truth is that such conversations make children extremely anxious. Instead, in discussing sexual infidelity, the explanation that "Mommy doesn't love Daddy anymore; she loves somebody else and wants to be with him" is straightforward and accurate.

In cases where the divorce is by mutual consent, you might open the discussion by explaining that "Mommy and Daddy don't love each other now. They don't want to live together anymore." This should be followed by telling the children enough details so that the reality of the situation is impressed on them. These details will also help the children to know that, while certain things are changing for them, the changes are such that they can understand and cope with.

Thus, if one parent is moving out of the house, the children should be told where that parent will be living. If at all possible, they should be taken to see the parent's new home. They should be told when they will see the absent parent, and under what conditions.

Such details are very important because young children think in concrete, not abstract, terms. It is impossible for a very young child to hear a general statement like "Daddy's gone away" without fearing that his father may have disappeared forever. It is crucial for the child to know *where* Daddy is going, and *when* he will be able to visit him.

What about those cases in which one spouse actually abandons his or her spouse and children? Here the child is apt to be especially fearful that his remaining parent will also abandon him. He will need constant reassurance from the remaining parent that that parent still loves him and will not leave him.

In cases of actual abandonment, what is the child to be told?

Here I do not agree with the psychologists and psychiatrists who say the child should be told that Daddy (assuming, of course, it's the father who has gone) "has gone away and won't be back," and "Daddy doesn't love you anymore." I believe that these are fair answers, but only where the remaining parent *knows them to be true.* Many times, in cases of abandonment, the abandoning spouse will later try to communicate with, or even gain custody of, the child. Unless you are absolutely certain that the child's other parent will not reappear, you should admit the limits of your own knowledge.

In such a case, I believe that the only honest and fair way to answer the question "Is Daddy [or Mommy] coming back?" or

"Does Daddy love me?" is for the remaining parent to admit "I don't know." Certainly the child should never be told that the abandoning parent is dead. This sort of deceit can cause severe damage to a child, particularly if the "dead" parent should reappear at some later time.

On the other hand, there is nothing wrong with admitting that you simply don't know the answer. The child can accept an answer like "I don't know if Daddy's coming back. I don't think he'll be back," or "I don't know if Daddy loves you. He doesn't act as though he loves you when he goes away." If the remaining parent is otherwise calm when she gives these answers, and doesn't indicate that she herself is in a panic, the child can appreciate and accept that degree of uncertainty.

Similarly, the child can be made to understand certain other truths concerning his parents' separation. If the marriage is ending because one partner has become an alcoholic, or has been heavily involved with drugs, or has a serious psychiatric disorder, it is impossible, and inadvisable, to attempt to protect your child from this knowledge. The child has already seen his parent drunk or drugged, or has already witnessed parental arguments and conflict over these problems. He knows something is very wrong. The kindest, and healthiest, thing to do under the circumstance is to help the child understand the nature of his parent's problem.

It is in the best interest of the child for the problem to be explained in such a way that he understands that the afflicted parent is "sick" rather than "bad." Explanations should be kept simple. Statements such as "Mommy has a sickness that makes her drink too much" may start the discussion. Any questions that the children may have should be answered honestly. It is far better to inform your children than to leave them defenseless against their own fears and the questions and cruel remarks of others.

Nowadays, one hears of an increasingly discussed reason for the breakup of a marriage: the homosexuality of one parent. There is still a lot of misunderstanding about homosexuality, and many parents are particularly reluctant to discuss this subject with their children. For one thing, many parents belong to religious denominations that have grave strictures against the practice of homosexuality, regarding it as a sin. Others fear that exposing their child even to the idea of homosexuality may somehow turn the child into a homosexual.

There is certainly no evidence to prove that educating your child about homosexuality exposes him to a greater risk of engaging in homosexual behavior. Neither is there evidence suggesting that the child of a homosexual parent is more likely than the child of a heterosexual to become homosexual himself. It should also be pointed out that the American Psychiatric Association no longer considers unconflicted homosexuality to be a psychiatric illness.

When a marriage ends because of the homosexuality of a parent, the child should be told. Otherwise, she will learn about it anyway, in time, and probably in ways that will confuse and distress her. For young children, the explanation may be kept simple: "Daddy doesn't love Mommy anymore. He wants to love men instead." For some older children, especially adolescents, educational literature may be helpful.

I realize this advice may be troubling to some parents. But I do believe that an effort should be made to keep concepts like "sin" and "sickness" out of the discussion when explaining homosexuality to a child. The child, in growing, will eventually come to his own conclusions on this topic. Meanwhile, one parent should not denigrate the other before the child.

Perhaps the hardest questions to answer occur when one parent genuinely appears to lack all interest in the child. When it becomes apparent that one spouse simply does *not* seem to love his child, it is best to be honest with the child about this. Again, the child will probably already have sensed her parent's lack of interest. In this case, it is important to emphasize to the child that the parent's lack of concern is not due to any unlovability on the child's part, but to some sort of lack in the parent. You might explain that "Something's wrong with Daddy. He can't love you. It's not your fault."

It is also important to tell your child that Mommy and Daddy did love each other when they were married and when the child was conceived. The child must know that she was wanted, and that she was a product of love.

How should you expect your children to react when you tell them of the divorce? Reactions will differ, according to the child's age and individual temperament. Partly, the child's reaction will be influenced by your own.

Many parents are afraid they will upset their children by displaying their own feelings at this time. Anger, frustration, fear, and grief are normal reactions to the breakup of a marriage. My own judgment is that children should not be protected from these feelings. It is a part of growing up to learn to understand and appreciate the feelings of others. Watching their parents cry or express anger or frustration will impress upon the children the fact that parents, too, have feelings that merit consideration.

In fact, children are apt to be more puzzled by the *absence* of emotion in a parent than by a display of feeling. The parents of eight-year-old Billy went out of their way to act as if nothing had happened. Their unnatural calm and false cheerfulness only seemed to confuse the boy, making it harder for him to accept the news. His reaction, described later, was "Why are Mommy and Daddy saying they won't be living together anymore? There's nothing wrong." In this case, a more open show of emotions — anger, sadness, upset — would have helped the boy to comprehend the truth.

I must, however, add one warning. While it is good for children to see that their parents, too, have feelings, it can be very frightening for a small child to see his parent "fall apart." In other words, it is not good for a young child to see his parent totally out of control, completely hysterical or enraged. To a young child the parent represents order, rules, authority. A young child who sees his parents lose all self-control, becoming totally paralyzed with grief or indulging in verbal or physical violence, may imagine that the world — literally — is coming apart. He cannot separate his parents' behavior from the rest of the world; his parents' actions take on global implications. A breakdown of all control on his parents' part can be terrifying to a child.

Where, then, is a parent to draw the line? This is a difficult time for parents, and many parents will not always be able to protect their children from highly emotional scenes. You must use your own best judgment concerning when you feel able to discuss divorce with your child. Again, I must stress that tears and controlled expressions of anger are to be expected — from both parents and child — during such discussions. Very hysterical or violent behavior is to be avoided, if at all possible.

What sort of reactions should you expect from your child when you tell him of the divorce? First, of course, will come the obvious question, "Why?" But these "whys?" may come in different ways, and over a period of time.

Some parents are puzzled by the child's apparent lack of interest in this very important news. "Our six-year-old didn't even seem interested," complained one mother. "He just wanted to go watch his favorite television program."

There are many possible reasons for such a reaction. First of all, we must recognize that children have very limited attention spans. This span, of course, will vary according to the child's age. But young children, especially, are simply unable to retain too much information in one period. For these children, it is probably best to feed information in small quantities. For example, you could start by saying, "Mommy and Daddy aren't going to live together anymore. Daddy won't be living here; he's going somewhere else." This might be all the information your child can handle at that moment. Later, he will have many more "whys?" about the details of the divorce.

Children of all ages may feign lack of interest or curiosity in the divorce for another reason: They may be afraid to verbalize their fantasies and fears. They may sense that the parents find their questions embarrassing. Parents may unwittingly add to this feeling by being curt with the children, or by avoiding their questions. Instead, you should encourage their questions, with such statements as "I know that our divorce is very important to you, and very confusing. I want to answer your questions about it whenever I can." It will be much easier for children to accept this great change in their lives if they feel all of their questions will willingly be answered.

Children, especially young children, may also be afraid to ask about the divorce because they feel responsible for it. (We have already discussed the way in which egocentricity in children leads them to distort their true role in certain events.) Many children will feel that they are to blame for their parents' separation. In such a case, the child will often be afraid to ask questions about the divorce. He may secretly fear that the answers will confirm that the divorce was "his fault."

I cannot overemphasize how important it is to reassure your child, at every stage of the separation and divorce, that the divorce was the result of the parents' choice, and not the result of the child's "bad" thoughts or actions. Such fears are common even in older children. It is important to know that your child may have these fears, even though he never openly expresses them.

Finally, there is another common reaction that a child may

bring to news of his parents' divorce: a seeming obsession with "selfish" details. We have touched on this problem already. It is good to remember, though, that the child whose only concern seems to be "Will I still have my birthday party?" or "Will Daddy take me to the movies?" is trying, in his own way, to understand and master a difficult emotional situation. Such concrete details are the only emotional handle the child may be able to grasp at first.

Explaining separation and divorce to a child cannot really be done in one session, or over a period of a few days. The child's ability to understand these events will grow as she grows. The child may continue to have questions long after the divorce. We will now see how you can help your child in the post-divorce period.

3

Games Parents Play

A DIVORCE DECREE marks the legal end of a marriage as that marriage is recognized by the state. But a husband and wife have much more than a merely legal status. They were, at one time, deeply in love. They share a common history, common friendships. And most important, they share the parenthood of their children, for whose physical and emotional welfare they are still responsible.

None of these important shared experiences can be magically erased by a legal document. Former spouses simply cannot erase the memories of their years together, whether they were good years or bad.

Divorce, then, does not truly *end* the relationship between a man and woman; it merely changes that relationship. Former spouses will still have feelings about each other. And, if they have children whom they both care about, the parents will of necessity have to deal with each other after the divorce, on matters affecting the children. The manner in which parents treat each other on these occasions will greatly affect the attitudes and emotional growth of their children.

Some divorced parents end their marriage with relatively little acrimony, or manage to overcome their negative feelings after a cooling-off period following the divorce. They maintain an active interest in each other's welfare and may even see each other socially from time to time. On some level, these divorced couples still seek and need the concern and even the approval of their former spouses.

In fact, divorced parents frequently feel a need to maintain some sort of contact with each other after the divorce. But these needs are not always healthy, and the contacts can sometimes be very destructive.

To understand this, we may have to rethink the meaning of the word *need*. In childhood, we all have an overwhelming need for the love and approval of our parents. If, for some reason, we feel that such love is being denied us, we may seek attention in negative ways, by behaving badly. To a child, and to many adults, any sort of attention, however negative, is far preferable to being totally ignored. A child who feels ignored by his parents may go out of his way to do something that he knows will arouse his parents' wrath and result in his own punishment.

Many children who have formed a tendency to attract negative attention carry this trait into their adult relationships. For reasons too complicated to explain here, they derive great emotional satisfaction from the attention their own spouses show when they allow themselves to become engaged in constant vicious argument. Not surprisingly, marriages of this sort frequently end in divorce.

But in many cases the relationship does not end at that point. The fighting continues after the divorce. The possible topics for argument are numerous: alimony, child support, visitation, and child-rearing practices, among them. This continued fighting — and it can go on for years after the divorce — satisfies the neurotic need of both former spouses to engage each other's attention. Unfortunately, since their children are now the main thing these two people have in common, it is the children who become the subject — and victims — of these arguments.

Six-year-old Michael was one child who found himself constantly involved in his parents' endless quarreling. Typically, Michael's father would arrive late on his appointed visiting day, which would frustrate Michael's mother, who had usually made plans to use the free time for her own recreational purposes. Michael's mother would then criticize the father: his mode of dress, the company he kept, the "evil influences" to which Michael was exposed while in his father's company. The father in turn, would criticize his ex-wife for being a "religious nut." There was literally no end to the subjects these two could argue about, because there was no end to their need to abuse each other and to be abused.

While Michael's parents may have been satisfying their own needs, they were doing enormous harm to their child. For one thing, since Michael served as the focal point of these arguments, the child became convinced that he was indeed the cause of his parents' divorce. "If they hadn't had me, they wouldn't always be fighting," he reasoned.

Second, Michael's parents were providing the little boy with a model of the way men and women behave together, and this model was far from healthy. Mothers and fathers are, to a small child, the most important example of interaction between the sexes, and the fact of divorce does not change this. The child who witnesses only anger and verbal violence between his parents is apt to grow up thinking that this is the way all men and women behave together. Naturally, under these circumstances, the child may learn to fear or distrust the opposite sex. These feelings and attitudes can be carried on through later life, and may seriously affect the child's later attitudes toward romantic love, courtship, and marriage.

Finally, there is one aspect to the fighting between Michael's parents that may seem strange at first. That is, this constant arguing actually encouraged Michael's reconciliation fantasies about his parents. I know it seems odd to think that such hostile interchanges could encourage a child to think that his parents might reunite. But as we now know, reconciliation fantasies are very strong in children of Michael's age. And — this is important to remember — any sort of prolonged and intense relationship between the child's parents can only encourage the child in such fantasies.

Michael's parents may have been abusive to each other, but no one witnessing their constant arguments could doubt the intensity, however, negative, of their feelings. It was clear that, in a heavily neurotic way. Michael's parents still needed each other and relied heavily on each other. Michael, like most children, was sensitive enough to feel the intensity of this bond between his parents. Their evident need for each other led him to hope that they could come to love each other again.

We see, then, that the evolving relationship of the parents after divorce and their attitude toward each other will profoundly affect the child. But, though parents may have the best of intentions concerning their future relationship with their ex-spouses, other factors may be at work that serve to make the situation less than ideal. This is because parents, like their children, are likely to be profoundly and negatively affected by the divorce.

For one thing, newly divorced parents may find themselves in very different financial circumstances, having to adjust to a new lifestyle. A mother may be forced to move back into her own parents' house. She may, with little training or skill, be forced for the first time to look for a job. A father who wins custody of the children may suddenly feel overwhelmed with the new responsibilities of child rearing.

In addition, the newly divorced parent may be subject to bouts of intense loneliness. He or she may be unsure of his newly changed social status. The custodial parent, in particular, may have great difficulty in satisfying his or her social or sexual needs while coping with the suddenly intensified demands of single parenthood.

All of these illustrations are meant to point up one important fact: The newly divorced parent will very likely find himself or herself under considerable emotional strain. Such a parent may be subject to periods of intense sadness or even bouts of severe depression. Depression, which is not an uncommon reaction to divorce, can be intensified if the divorce involves a dramatic change in lifestyle as, for example, a sudden and sharp reduction in income. Most depressions are self-limiting and will clear up in due time. In severe and prolonged cases, professional help should be sought.

But a parent's depression or other form of emotional upset following a divorce will necessarily affect the parent's relationship with her child. For one thing, the depressed person ordinarily has lost interest in life and is unable to involve herself with people and events around her. Thus, the depressed parent will often appear to be less interested in her child, less responsive to his needs, and less accessible to him. In the most severe cases of depression, the parent may take to bed and be unable even to feed or care for the child. But even in more common or milder cases, the parent may find it difficult to pay close attention and to respond to the child's needs. This does *not* mean that the depressed parent is unfeeling; it is simply a manifestation of a depressed state.

Not all newly divorced parents suffer from significant depression. But all can expect to have to cope with difficult emotions — anger, confusion, a sense of being overwhelmed — in the months after the divorce.

It is important to realize that parents, at this time, will have their own emotional needs, needs that are separate, and sometimes quite different, from those of the child. But all too often, a parent may unwittingly use the child to meet his own needs, hindering the child in his own struggle to make a healthy adjustment to the divorce.

One example of this occurs when the parent, particularly the depressed parent, unconsciously encourages the child to persist in unhealthy behavior he might otherwise grow out of. Often a child will experience certain behavioral problems in the immediate post-divorce period. Most often, however, these symptoms will disappear after a time. The child may, for example, experience a period of bed-wetting, or school problems, or may himself appear to be depressed. The parent who is caught up in his own emotional problems and who refuses to try to overcome them, may be unconsciously gratified by the child's behavior. On some level, the parent may actually signal to the child his approval of that behavior. The child's problems, in this instance, serve to confirm the parent's view that the divorce was a great catastrophe, that his entire world has collapsed, that the situation is hopeless. In fact, this sort of behavior on a parent's part can contribute to the child's maladjustment, not only in the immediate post-divorce period, but throughout later life. The custodial parent may then use the child's continuing problem in an attempt to hurt the ex-spouse. "Look how sad [or sickly, or angry] little Joey has been since the divorce," the parent can say. "It's all your fault."

There are many other ways in which the emotionally needy parent can unwittingly interfere with the child's healthy adjustment to divorce. One of the most common is for the newly divorced custodial mother to tell her young son, "You're the man of the house now. I have to rely on you," or "Now that Daddy's gone, you must be like a father to your little brothers and sisters." Similarly, the father who has custody of his daughter may put her in the wife-housekeeper-mother role, making her responsible for the care of her younger brothers and sisters and for the major housekeeping chores. Unconsciously, the parent may place his opposite-sex child in the role of grownup, or worse, of spouse.

Parents should be very careful to avoid falling into such dependency on their children. No matter how lovingly intended, this treatment can only harm the child. For one thing, it does not allow the child to act like a child. While children should be taught to accept responsibility around the house and may well benefit from helping with certain chores, particularly if the parent must also work outside the home, this is a far cry from demanding that the child act like a grownup. It is easy for the child to feel overwhelmed by such demands, particularly in the period immediately following the divorce. After all, the child should feel free to express the reactions that are natural for her immature state of development. Twelve-year-old Alexa, however, was denied this freedom and was forced into a role beyond her years.

Alexa's parents had divorced two years earlier. After her mother took a sales job requiring a great deal of travel, she agreed to give custody of Alexa and her younger sister and brother to their father. Alexa's father loved his children but knew nothing about running a household or cooking meals. Increasingly, Alexa began to assume the tasks her mother had always performed: cooking, doing laundry, cleaning house. She was also responsible for looking after the younger children after school and even helping them with their schoolwork. The younger children began to regard Alexa almost as a mother, and her father bragged about how she was "mature beyond her years." Eager to please the father she adored, Alexa made no complaint about her daily routine. Until a teacher at school pointed it out to him, her father did not notice that Alexa often seemed unnaturally quiet, and that she had become almost totally isolated from girls of her own age.

Alexa's case is not uncommon. While it was certainly reasonable for her to assume some responsibility for the housework, it was entirely wrong for anyone to expect her to become, at age twelve, homemaker for her father and mother to her brother and sister. Always caring for someone else, Alexa was never given the opportunity to express her own feelings or to look to someone older for advice. For a young girl on the edge of adolescence to suppress all those feelings and questions and to have to play grownup can be damaging indeed. Parents should be very careful not to place too much responsibility on the shoulders of a child.

There is another, even more compelling, reason why you should not overestimate the maturity of your opposite-sex children after the divorce. As I have noted, there is an understandable temptation for the newly divorced custodial mother to rely very heavily on her oldest son for support during this period, just as the custodial father often comes to rely on his daughter. Such parents often fall into the trap of viewing these children as surrogate spouses. But the son who hears his mother call him "the man of the house" or the daughter who becomes the "little mother" may suffer severe anguish and confusion, not to mention guilt regarding their feelings toward their parents.

I have already spoken of the oedipal phase which most children go through from the ages of three to five. Children during the oedipal phase develop very strong loving feelings for their opposite-sex parent and commonly wish that the same-sex parent would go away so that the child may have the opposite-sex parent all to himself. I also explained that the child usually feels guilt or fear regarding his "competition" with the same-sex parent. Eventually, these feelings are resolved when the child decides to imitate his same-sex parent and look for another person of the opposite sex on whom to concentrate his romantic or sexual feelings.

Although the oedipal phase is at its most intense when the child is very young, some of these oedipal feelings continue in the child up to and including adolescence. It is common knowledge, in many families, that fathers and daughters are especially devoted to each other, as are mothers and sons. There is nothing wrong with these feelings. In fact, in the healthy family, they can and will help the child to grow and develop his sense of self-esteem.

But we must understand that, in these intense father-daughter and mother-son relationships, there are necessarily some elements of romantic or sexual feeling. All of us, children and adults, are sexual beings, and it is impossible to divorce all sexual elements from feelings of intense love or romance. Sexual feelings are normal. But that does not mean that all sexual feelings must, or should, be acted upon. Recent studies indicate that incest — overt sexual behavior between parents and children or between brothers and sisters — may be more widespread in this country than was previously suspected. Evidence also points to the fact that children who are engaged in incest, even if they appear to have consented to the act, are gravely damaged by the experience. Many such children later find it impossible to function normally in adult life.

This discussion of incest is certainly not intended to frighten away an affectionate parent or to make you withdraw warmth and approval from your opposite-sex child. It is just to remind you to be aware that there may no longer be the same safeguards that exist in the normal, intact family that prevent these universal child-parent sexual feelings from being acted upon. These safeguards are sometimes referred to as incest taboos. Ordinarily, they work on such an unconscious and automatic level that we are not even aware of them.

For example, studies have shown that mothers spend less time physically stroking and fondling their infant sons than they do their infant daughters. With fathers, the result was just the opposite: Fathers spend less time touching their baby daughters. Interviews with the parents later showed that they were unaware of this pattern in their behavior. These patterns continue as the child grows. Most parents, for example, have less and less extended physical contact with the opposite-sex child as the child grows older. And as the child begins to develop sexually, he or she will ordinarily begin to demand more privacy when bathing or dressing.

What does all this discussion of sexual feelings within a family have to do with the post-divorce situation? Simply this: Though the normal child has some degree of romantic or sexual feeling toward his opposite-sex parent, those feelings are usually safely buried away under the usual sexual taboos that most families observe. These taboos are necessary for the child, particularly the adolescent, whose sexual feelings are more defined. Ordinarily, the child is able to repress such feelings, or to deny their existence. This denial is really a healthy mechanism. If the child were to be confronted with the reality of these sexual feelings, he would ordinarily feel enormously guilty — "dirty" and "evil." This is particularly true of adolescents who, under even the best of circumstances, are having a difficult time trying to cope with the now overt, unmistakable signs of their sexuality.

The child who is left in the custody of the opposite-sex parent may thus face a special problem. He no longer has the presence of the same-sex parent in the family household to encourage him to repress his sexual feelings toward his now-custodial parent, and thus be spared the pain of acknowledging them.

Let's take Alexa's situation. Alexa was twelve years old, the age of puberty, a time when a young girl is particularly sensitive and vulnerable to problems concerning sex and sexual feelings. She was deeply devoted to her father, with whom she had a healthy and loving relationship. Like many normal loving daughters, she often had possessive feelings about her father, wishing she had him all to herself. And at times, like any normal adolescent daughter, she felt herself to be in competition with her mother.

None of these feelings bothered Alexa very much, because

they were made harmless and impossible by the reality of the situation: that her father really belonged only to her mother.

When Alexa's parents were divorced, and her mother moved out of the house, Alexa faced a problem that we discussed in chapter 1. That is, she felt somehow that she had done something evil by forcing her mother out of the house and winning her father all to herself. Ordinarily, Alexa may well have been able to overcome these normal and transitory guilt feelings. But Alexa's father greatly complicated the situation by putting his own emotional needs ahead of his daughter's. The father, who before the divorce had had little to do with the day-to-day tasks of raising children and running a household, turned to Alexa as his main source of advice and emotional support. He complained to the girl about his hurt and loneliness at his wife's departure. He consulted her on the training and discipline of his younger children. He confided in her his small successes and failures at the office, even, on occasion, asking her advice about his own problems.

What Alexa's father was doing, unconsciously, was using her as a surrogate wife, as an emotional crutch to get himself through a difficult time.

But a child nearly always knows when he or she is being used as a surrogate spouse, and the experience can have very serious adverse consequences for the child. At first, Alexa was gratified by her father's attentions, enjoying the special status and grown-up role of housekeeper, mother, and confidante. But inevitably as Alexa became aware that her father regarded her as more than just a daughter, she was reminded of her own romantic feelings toward him. In reaction to these thoughts, she became very anxious and found it increasingly difficult to function in her daily life.

Eventually, after a very unhappy period, both Alexa and her father sought out professional counseling. Alexa, in time, learned to be more accepting of her own sexuality. More important,

Alexa's father learned to treat her in ways appropriate to her age and to establish other supportive relationships with adult friends and lovers.

I have emphasized this problem of the surrogate spouse because it is very common, and one that can do great harm to a child. While children of every age are vulnerable to the surrogate-parent problem, teen-agers often seem most sensitive to it.

I would be remiss if I did not point out one manifestation of this problem that seems to exist most frequently between mothers and their sons — that is, a common tendency among newly divorced mothers to develop a rather flirtatious relationship with their sons. Nearly all of this behavior is unconscious on the mother's part, and nearly all of these mothers will flatly deny such behavior if it is pointed out to them. Normally, the behavior is quite mild, consisting of remarks such as "You're the man of the house now," or "I'll have to depend on you now, the way I did on your father." And ordinarily, this behavior stems from the mother's emotional needs, rather than from any overtly sexual motives.

But I have seen cases where the parent's behavior goes quite beyond the remarks noted above. Often, in so-called liberated or open households, parents often show themselves naked before their opposite-sex teen-age children, when bathing or dressing. I do not know whether this is a healthy development in an intact home. But I do know that where a father, for example, has left the home, and a teen-age son is left to work out a relationship with his newly divorced mother, such provocative behavior on the mother's part can seriously damage the son. Most teen-agers, at this stage, have a great need to deny their parents' sexuality completely. The flaunting of sexual behavior by a parent can arouse intense anxiety in the teen-ager.

So far in this chapter I have discussed the surrogate-spouse problem mainly as it would affect teen-agers. That is because of the evidence that, in the adolescent years, children are particularly sensitive to these situations. But what has been said here can be applied to a child of almost any age. Since the surrogate-parent situation creates anxieties arising out of the oedipal conflict, which begins around the age of three, any little boy above that age can feel conflict and guilt if he is made to feel that he has replaced his father in his mother's eyes. The same holds true, of course, for any little girl.

We have already seen, then, several ways in which the emotional needs of a parent after divorce, if not handled properly, can harm the child's own adjustment to the situation. There is another, even more direct way in which parental feelings can harm the child. This occurs, and not infrequently, when a parent actually blames the child as being the cause of the divorce. At first, it may seem ridiculous to blame a child for the end of a marriage. Yet such accusations are not uncommon, and children who are the victims of this type of parental blame can suffer severe and lasting psychological damage.

This situation usually arises when one parent (for this example, we will use the mother) has resisted the divorce and feels herself to be still very much in love with her ex-spouse. Typically, however, such a person has been living in a world of her own, refusing, usually for years, to acknowledge the mounting evidence that her marriage is in a shambles. She may deny evidence of her husband's infidelity, or drinking, of her own equally serious problems. She may insist, up to the divorce itself, that she has a perfect marriage.

How can a person be so oblivious to reality? There are many possible explanations. Some people are so abnormally egocentric that they literally cannot pay much attention to the world around them, including their families. Other people live in a neurotic world of fantasy, unable to distinguish the perfect fantasy from the less-than-perfect truth. Others employ the defense mechanism called denial. We have already noted how certain children may, at least initially, deny to themselves and others the fact of their parents' divorce. But it is not uncommon for an ex-spouse to be so traumatized and guilty about divorce as to deny the real causes for it. Ironically, it is most often when an ex-spouse feels insecure about having done something to cause the divorce that he or she will openly blame someone else for the end of the marriage.

When that someone else happens to be the child, the parent's blame may be either open or disguised. The parent may simply complain about "how hard it is to raise children" or talk about "all the sacrifices your father and I had to make for you." Or she may come right out and tell the child, "Before you were born, your father and I never had any problems." Indeed, from the embittered mother's standpoint, that latest statement may be true. Very often, in the pre-children, honeymoon phase of a marriage, latent problems have not had time to surface, and other areas of tension — finances, sexual behavior, lifestyle roles — have not had time to develop. There is also no doubt that the addition of children to a family changes the expectations and the responsibilities of the parents. In any case, the fault lies, not in the children themselves, but in the parents' immaturity and inability to accept their responsibilities as parents.

Children, because they engage in magical thinking, are already prone to feel themselves responsible, to some degree, for their parents' divorce. When a parent exaggerates these feelings by letting the child think he is indeed at fault, he is not only telling the child that he is "evil," but also, in effect, that he is unloved. I'm sure that I don't have to describe the grave harm that such treatment can do to even the sturdiest child. Often such children will need intensive and expert professional help to restore their self-esteem.

There are a few very sad — and emotionally very complicated — cases in which one parent will in fact leave the family because of a child. This occurs in certain instances when the child is severely and permanently handicapped, either emotionally or physically. These are very delicate and fairly unique situations. It is difficult for an outsider to pass judgment on the parent who decides to leave his family under these circumstances. Rather, our concern should be with the parent who remains, and with the disabled child and his siblings. In these situations, it is especially important to reassure the disabled child that she retains the love of those around her. It might be explained that "Daddy [or Mommy] left us because he didn't want to be a part of our family anymore. He can't live with us. It's not our fault."

Also, I encourage single parents who are raising disabled children to contact one or more of the many self-help and support groups that have sprung up to help such families in the last few years. Single parents in such a situation face a formidable task, and it is important that they find their own sources of emotional support.

Thus far we have discussed the immediate post-divorce period and the very intense parental emotional states that affect the child during this period. As time passes, both children of divorce and their parents will likely grow used to — and make peace with — their changed circumstances. If the parents can reach an amicable state, or at least a truce, with each other, then of course emotional pressures on the children will be greatly relieved.

As so often happens, here again, parents are faced with the choice of whose needs to put first: their own need to continue hostilities with their ex-spouse or the need of their children to grow up with healthy adult role models. It is certainly possible for a former husband and wife to continue a hostile and bitter relationship for years, or indeed for a lifetime.

I ask you to remember, however, that even after your divorce, you and your ex-spouse will continue to be, in your children's eyes, a most important model for male-female relationships. To an astonishing degree, children take from their parents some of their most important lessons about how to treat the opposite sex in their own lives. It is inevitable, and necessary, that children will learn that adults are sometimes cruel to each other, even, on occasion, to those they love. It is not necessary that children be exposed to pitched battles between their parents after a divorce. Parents who cannot maintain amicable, or at least civil, contact with each other after the divorce, should keep these contacts to a minimum.

Undeniably, there are divorce situations in which one partner has behaved less than nobly. In these cases, there will be a great deal of legitimate anger during and after the divorce. No doubt the children will early become aware of this anger and the reasons for it. If the children themselves were injured by the parents' actions — physically abused, for example, or neglected — the children will feel hostile and betrayed. If one parent badly brutalized the other, physically or mentally, the children's protective instincts may make them equally hostile and resentful.

There are two important things for the custodial parent to remember here (assuming that the noncustodial parent is the one who has behaved badly). The first has to do with the child's possible wish to reconcile with the offending parent. Such a wish may well develop after the first intense feeling of the immediate post-divorce period. Here, again, the custodial parent must put the child's interests before his own. I feel very strongly that, unless the custodial parent has *real reason* to believe that the child's renewed contact with the other parent will result in genuine harm to *the child,* reconciliation should be encouraged.

What is "genuine harm" to the child, in this case? A common example of a problem here occurs where the ex-husband professes love for and a strong desire to visit regularly with his children. Yet this same man commonly misses making his child-support payments, often without excuse. In most instances, unless the male parent is actually unemployed or insolvent, his failure to make child-support payments is a weapon that he uses against his ex-wife. Often, such a man will claim that, unless he holds back the payments, his former wife will forbid him access to the children altogether. The ex-wife will argue, on the other hand, that her refusal to allow the father to see his children is her only inducement to get him to make the child-support payments. She may also withhold the children from their father if he makes child-support payments but does not keep up with alimony payments.

In the case of alimony payments, I believe that a child should be allowed, if he wishes, to visit the father since any harm or cruelty of which the father may be guilty is directed at his former wife, not at his children.

In the case of child-support payments, of course, the child's welfare is being more directly affected. It can be argued that the father *is* harming the child, and that his children should be kept from him. Under these circumstances, if the children understand the situation and still want to reconcile with their father, I believe they should be allowed to do so. Certainly the child should first be told the truth: Daddy is no longer paying their expenses and this has made the mother's situation more difficult. If the child, understanding this, still wants to see his father, the mother has, I believe, no right to keep father and child apart.

I realize that this advice may seem terribly unfair to the working mother who is struggling to keep financially afloat, while her ex-husband refuses to meet his own financial obligations to the family. But the question, in this and similar situations, which the ex-husband or ex-wife must ask himself or herself is this: What is this disagreement really about? Is it possible that my ex-spouse and I are inadvertently hurting our children because we're so intent on hurting each other? In most cases, no matter what the subject matter of the argument, the answer to that question is yes.

What I am stressing here is simply that the child's good should be the first consideration. What I am asking the parent to do is extremely difficult; I'm well aware of the intensity of the animosities and feelings that can build up between divorced parents. Why, then, do I lean toward the encouragement of reconciliation between children and parents who may have in some way hurt them, and who are sorry for that hurt?

The main consideration here, to my mind, is the healthy psychological development of the child. It is of primary importance that the child grow up with loving, caring role models of both sexes. We will discuss this in more detail in the next chapter. Let me here just note the obvious: The little girl who never sees her father, who hears constantly from her embittered mother that "all men are bums," and who has no close, positive, male role models may well have substantial difficulty in relating to the opposite sex when she matures. It is important that children have consistent contact with positive opposite-sex role models.

The important question then, is not: "Does my ex-husband like me?" It is: "Does he love the children and want to be with them?" If the answer to that second question is yes and the parent's time with his children is rewarding to them, one does the children a grave disservice in denying them his company. In fact, if you can let your ex-spouse know that you want him, not just to pay his children's expenses, but to be an important part of their lives, you may actually find that your own relationship with each other improves.

Even when all technical visitation questions have been settled, and even at times when parents seem to be enjoying an amicable relationship, there is one other destructive game they play with their children. Most often, parents are not really aware of the nature or repercussions of this game, or even that they are play-ing it at all. I am referring to one parent's use of the child to inform on the other parent. This typically occurs when the child returns from a weekend visit with his father. By Monday morning, the mother may be full of questions, ranging from "Does Daddy keep his new house neat?" to "Does Daddy have any special girl friends?" Such questions are bound to make the child uneasy; at best, they give the child the unmistakable impression that he is telling on his father.

It is natural for one ex-spouse to be curious about the current life of the other, and the child, if he or she sees both parents regularly, is a veritable gold mine of this sort of information. Consequently, a parent may think it very innocent to question his child on "Mommy's social life." But this is never an innocent activity; your child will feel, quite reasonably, that he is being used as an informer, and may feel torn between the disloyalty of telling the secrets of one parent versus the pressure of refusing to tell the other.

Of course, this situation becomes much more strained when the relationship between the ex-spouses is very stormy. Ten-year-old Tom, who lived with his father, faced such a problem. Tom's parents made no secret of their outright hatred for each other. His father called his mother, who had had several affairs, a whore. His mother retaliated by calling the father, who fre-quented bars, a drunken bum.

After Tom's weekend visits with his mother, the father would castigate her to the boy, asking if there had been "men in Mommy's bedroom." When the mother saw Tom, she similarly grilled him about his father's behavior.

Tom loved both of his parents, but this situation created in-tolerable conflicts for him. To keep his father's love, he felt that he had to report on his mother's behavior, and agree that she was a "bad woman." To keep his mother's love, he had to express similar negative feelings about his father. Tom felt guilty and insecure and disloyal all the time; he also lived in fear that his parents would find out his true feelings and stop loving him. These conflicts affected the boy's behavior so severely that his parents were forced, finally, to get him professional help.

In psychotherapy it very soon became clear that Tom's problems — which included school truancy and poor peer relationships — were caused by the intolerable pressures created by his parents' actions. However, neither parent would accept the child psychologist's explanation of the problem or his recommendation that the parents themselves enter therapy to examine their own behavior. Thus, while Tom's psychologist was able to aid the boy somewhat by helping him understand his own feelings, he could do nothing to change the parental behavior that was the true cause of the boy's distress. This, unfortunately, is not an uncommon outcome in cases like this.

I have tried to outline some of the ways in which a parent's feelings may unintentionally injure the child in the immediate post-divorce period. Let us see now how the formal structuring of the child's parental contacts — custody and visitation — affect the child.

4

Custody and Visitation

WE HAVE CONSIDERED how the parents' behavior in preparing the child for the fact of divorce can have a great effect on the child's adjustment. And we have seen how the parents' feelings and problems in the immediate post-divorce period will necessarily involve the child. At these times, we know, parents must often place their own feelings and needs second to those of the child, who has fewer strengths and defenses with which to meet parental conflicts.

But what about that period of the actual legal process called "divorce"? The legal process, from the decision to separate to the formal granting of the final divorce decree, can take months or even, in some cases, years. This lengthy period would be of no particular significance if it involved only cool disinterested lawyers drawing up complicated but bloodless legal documents to be read and signed in the hushed and respectful atmosphere of a judge's chambers. But rarely, when a divorce involves children or property, is the process so cool and painless.

To be sure, many states have now adopted the so-called "no-fault" divorce law, which does away with the requirement that one partner be found guilty of adultery or some other offense before a divorce could be granted. This no-fault law spares many couples what used to be the staple of both gossip-column discussion and small-town community entertainment: agonizing public revelations concerning a divorcing couple's private lives and personal morality. We can only hope that all remaining states will follow suit in the near future with no-fault laws of their own.

But even the no-fault law is very far from removing all the pain from the legal divorce process. Even in so-called amicable divorces, there are issues to be resolved, issues that can result in a highly charged, emotional atmosphere. I am referring, of course, to the distribution of property, to alimony and child support, and most important, to child custody.

If the divorcing parents do not agree on one or more of these important issues, they must leave their resolution to the skill of their respective lawyers and to the wisdom of the court. Unfortunately, the entire design of our legal system — the so-called "adversary system" — does not work to the real advantage of any party in a divorce action. Rather, the system serves to maximize tension between the parties, sometimes even creating arguments out of issues that could have been settled peaceably.

The adversary system is part of our historical inheritance from the British common law. Under this system, a lawyer is ethically bound to use absolutely all of his skills and do everything ethically possible to win his client's cause. The opposing lawyer, of course, is completely and totally devoted to his own client's cause. The two lawyers thus tend to take extreme positions. The philosophy of the adversary system holds that, when two opposing positions are ably presented in court, the judge or jury will be able to sort through the extremes and come to the truth, which may well be somewhere in the middle.

The adversary system was developed centuries ago for use in criminal trials and some civil trials. It was not intended to be used in divorce cases, since these were originally handled in church courts. The adversary system, by encouraging divorcing parents to take extreme and unbending positions on such questions as child custody, can serve only to ensure the further deterioration of the relationship between the parents. More important, the emotional fallout from a protracted, hard-fought divorce suit can only harm the child.

Occasionally, of course, special circumstances force a long and hard-fought divorce litigation. Indeed, the intransigence of one of the parties (a flat refusal to allow the other parent to visit the children, for example, or a refusal to allow a reasonable property settlement) may literally force the other party to seek out the "toughest divorce lawyer in town." We have all seen, in movies or on television, how the toughest lawyer in town handles a case. If the divorce proceeds to the trial stage, he may put the opposing spouse on the witness stand. He may attempt to discredit him or her by asking pointed questions or dredging up unfavorable facts about the spouse's past life or personality, personal beliefs, or mental stability. Such experiences are far from pleasant either to witness or to endure, and they may dash any hope of an amicable relationship between the parties.

An even more appalling prospect is that of two aggressive lawyers examining and cross-examining the child. If there is clear hostility between the parents at this stage, the experience may be utterly horrible for the child. She will know that she is being asked to "tell secrets" about her parents, and in effect, to choose sides. There is no way in which the child can win in such a situation; she will feel guilty and miserable no matter what she says.

However, shouldn't the child, particularly the older child, have the chance during divorce proceedings to express her own views and preferences regarding custody and visitation? I believe so. But the potential for evoking guilt in the child in such circumstances are great. The child's thoughts and wishes should be elicited, but with care. The way *not* to do this is to put a child on a witness stand in open court. Indeed, I have often heard experienced trial judges note that the tension of testifying in open court sometimes reduces the most honest and mature citizen to a nervous wreck. How then, can one fully and objectively elicit the child's true thoughts?

Very often, a judge sitting in a divorce case will invite the child, particularly the older child, into the judge's chambers, where they can talk without the pressure of the parents' presence. However, even this is not always the perfect solution. In some instances, the child may have been coached by one parent concerning what to say. Even without such coaching, the child may feel reluctant to tell the judge which parent she prefers to live with. After all, chances are good that the child loves both parents to some degree, and her choice of one seems to involve an obvious rejection of the other.

This is an area in which professional psychological help can be very useful. In such a case, the psychologist or psychiatrist would intervene as a disinterested professional, to help discover the child's true feelings. Such a counselor would not put the child on the spot by demanding that he choose between parents. Rather, she would interview the child at length, about many things. She might join with him in certain games called "play therapy," in which the child reveals his thoughts and feelings. She might interview the child together with one or both parents, or with his entire family.

Based on these interviews, and perhaps on certain psychological tests, the psychologist or psychiatrist would then make a detailed report back to the judge of the divorce courts. This report is likely to be an accurate analysis of the child's thoughts and feelings, especially about custody. The court could then act, considering the psychological report as well as its own assessment of each parent's ability to raise the child.

The intervention of a counselor was particularly helpful in the case of ten-year-old Jane. Jane was of an age where judges commonly take into account the child's feelings regarding custody. (Unfortunately, some courts still do not consider the feelings of younger children.) In this case, the judge first put Jane on the witness stand, where she had to testify in front of her parents and the entire court. This had the effect of reducing the child to near-hysterics. Even later, in the privacy of the judge's chambers, Jane would not say a word to indicate her choice of the custodial parent. Instead, she would only say tearfully that she loved "both Mommy and Daddy."

Despite this, the judge was faced with the question of which parent to award custody to. Luckily, he was experienced enough in divorce matters to sense the strong sense of anguish and guilt that lay under Jane's outbursts. On his recommendation, the child was taken to a nearby clinic for a series of interviews and tests with an experienced psychiatric social worker.

In the course of these interviews, it became apparent that Jane was indeed deeply attached to both her mother and her father. It also became apparent that, at this particular time in her life, Jane felt an especially strong need for a warm and understanding father figure. Left to her own devices, she undoubtedly would have requested that the judge allow her to live with her father.

Unfortunately, Jane's mother, who was very much shaken by the divorce, had been innocently remarking to the girl that Jane was now "all she had" and "the only person she could rely on." Even at age ten, Jane could see that her mother was the weaker and more dependent of her parents. Knowing this, she felt too guilty to voice her preference for living with her father, thus "abandoning" her needy mother. Without psychological counseling, Jane's feelings would have remained hidden. Eventually, based on the psychological report and on the judge's evaluation of the father as a capable parent, Jane was sent to live with her father. On the advice of the social worker, the court allowed frequent and substantial visitation rights to Jane's mother, so that neither mother nor daughter would feel abandoned by the other.

Jane's case points up some problems commonly encountered by children during divorce proceedings. Jane, at age ten, was asked for her preference as to the custodial parent, and that preference was given considerable weight by the court. Most people — but by no means all — would agree that the feelings of a child of that age should be at least be considered.

But what about younger children? It is possible for psychiatrists and psychologists, working with a young child, to discover if a three- or four-year-old child has strong feelings in this area, and the reasons for those feelings. Certainly, in extreme cases, where the child has been abused by one parent, or forced to watch the abuse of one parent by the other, common sense dictates that the child's wish to avoid the offending parent be respected.

But beyond those dramatic cases, we approach a new area in both law and psychiatry. I confess that my own bias here is the traditional one: namely, that *unless there are special circumstances*, very young children are probably better off in the custody of their mothers. I realize that this may be becoming an unfashionable view, and I am willing to admit that there are many factors in our modern lifestyles that may qualify as special circumstances. Even so, the fact remains that, in the course of normal child development, the mother-infant ties that are born of biology and intensified by uniquely maternal nurturance (such as breast-feeding) are much more intense than the ties between father and child. These facts lead to an infant's uniquely important dependence on his mother. Consequently, children at least up to and including early school age are generally better off with their mother.

By and large, courts have followed this reasoning and have,

almost as a rule, awarded custody of young children to their mothers. This rule is now changing in some jurisdictions, and some fathers are receiving custody of their young children. But this still happens relatively rarely unless the father has clearly proven himself to be the superior parent. Even now divorced fathers receive custody of their children in only about 10 percent of all cases. While it is impossible to predict what direction the law will take in the near future, I believe that the presumption will remain, even if it is no longer spoken, that the mother is the more logical parent to raise the young child.

We have already seen that super-aggressive lawyers, and the adversarial legal system in general, may add greatly and unnecessarily to the tensions all parties feel during the divorce. This is particularly true when lawyers and judges pressure the child to choose between parents. In fact, no matter how this delicate question is handled, there is no perfect or painless solution to the problems of custody.

What, practically speaking, are custody and visitation rights likely to entail? There are, essentially, three types of child-custody arrangements, which can often be tailored to fit the needs of the individual case. The first, and traditionally the most common, form of custody arrangement is sole custody. Under sole custody, one parent is awarded the primary responsibility for raising all of his or her children. The children live permanently with the custodial parent, and generally, the court awards the noncustodial parent the right to visit the children at fixed times and for fixed periods. Visitation rights are rarely totally denied, except in extreme cases, such as child abuse. If there is much ill feeling and lack of cooperation between the parents, the visitation schedule will be drawn up by the court, which will rigidly enforce it. In these cases the court usually relies heavily on the advice of involved psychiatrists or social workers. When parents are able to cooperate with each other to serve the best interests of the child, the visitation schedule may be less rigid and more spontaneous.

Visitation practices vary considerably, depending in part on such factors as the emotional stability of both parent and child (for example, continuation of a clearly pathological parent-child relationship would clearly be damaging to the child) and realistic considerations of available time and geography (where, for instance, the noncustodial parent may have moved to a distant state). Typically the noncustodial parent may be allowed to see his child for part of each weekend and to have him for longer visits during school holidays and summer vacations. We will discuss possible problems and complications posed by visitation arrangements later on. But it is important to note here that, even in cases where one parent is awarded so-called sole custody, the court, by providing for visitation by the noncustodial parent, recognizes the very real need of the child for a continued loving relationship with both parents.

Until fairly recently, courts almost always awarded sole custody to one parent, and that parent was, in the overwhelming majority of cases, the mother. Today, however, other custody arrangements are gaining increasing favor. Some courts, in appropriate cases, will order "split custody" of the children. Another arrangement that has received wide publicity lately has been the relatively new concept of "joint custody."

Split custody is an arrangement whereby certain children of a divorced couple will live with their mother, while others will live with their father. There are both obvious advantages and disadvantages to such an arrangement. Generally speaking, in the absence of special circumstances, it is usually better for the children of a divorced couple to be kept together. For one thing, this helps children, especially young children, to maintain the concept that they are part of an ongoing entity — a family — that will remain central to their lives. As we have discussed, the children of a divorce often band together, comforting one another and drawing on one another for love and support. Not surprisingly, this often results in especially close and lasting ties among the children. Such closeness, surely, is to be encouraged. It seems especially unfortunate that children who are placed in split custody may, if one parent moves away, be separated by great physical distances and see each other only infrequently. There is also a danger, especially if such children are separated while still very young, that brothers and sisters may become more or less strangers to one another.

Still, there are cases in which a compelling argument can be made for split custody. For example, if all the children are adolescents, their own feelings about choosing a parent to live with will ordinarily be given great weight. Typically, some children of this age will simply get along better with their mothers, while others will feel more comfortable with their fathers. If both mother and father are found to be suitable parents, the children's wishes should be respected, even if it means the children will be separated.

Children of different ages and temperaments have individual needs that are sometimes clearly better served by one parent than the other. Such was the case in the Smith family. At the time of their divorce, the Smiths had three children: Carl, fifteen, Frannie, eleven, and two-year-old Billy. Mrs. Smith planned, after the divorce, to leave the small town in Indiana where the family had been living, and to settle in her parents' hometown in California. Both she and her ex-husband had petitioned the court for custody of all three children. The judge in this case agreed to take the wishes of the older children into account.

Their parents' separation presented Carl and Frannie with an especially difficult problem. Both children loved and respected both of their parents. But Carl, at fifteen, felt settled into the routine of his Indiana high school. He felt particularly close to his school friends and was especially proud of the fact that, after years of effort, he was beginning to excel in high school athletics. In this he had been greatly encouraged and aided by his father, a former college track star, who had for years patiently coached the boy. Carl had come to see his father as an important role model. As much as he loved his mother, he knew he could not leave both his father and his familiar surroundings.

Like Carl, eleven-year-old Frannie was reluctant to leave her familiar school and friends. But Frannie's needs and her personality were different from her brother's. For one thing, at age eleven, Frannie was beginning to experience the profound and sometimes confusing physical changes that are a part of a child's normal sexual development. Though her mother had carefully educated her about the process of sexual development, Frannie understandably looked to her mother as a model and for emotional support. At this age she had special questions, fears, and problems that she could never have comfortably brought to her father. In addition, Frannie was more extroverted than her brother and knew she would have little difficulty in making friends in a new school.

Two-year-old Billy was too young to understand the details of his parents' divorce or to consider the consequences of their living apart. Like most two-year-olds, however, Billy was intensely attached to his mother, who from his birth had been his primary caretaker. As is common in the case of very young children, the court ruled that Billy would remain with his mother.

But what of Carl and Frannie? After they had expressed their wishes in interviews with a social worker and, later, in private conversation with the judge, the judge respected the wishes of both children: Carl was allowed to remain with his father, and Frannie to stay with her mother.

This solution, although probably the best one in these circumstances, was not without its problems. Often, split-custody cases leave both parents and children with painful feelings of guilt or regret. Inevitably, split custody does result in the physical breakup of a family. The child who chooses to live with one parent will almost inevitably feel some guilt about rejecting the other. In addition, he must face the fact that his decision means that he will be separated from his siblings, whom he may love deeply.

Parents must handle the split-custody situation with great delicacy and understanding. The parent not chosen by his child will be tempted to express his anger and grief at the child's "rejection." Such displays of feeling on the parent's part only serve to increase the child's sense of guilt and trauma. Physical distance may then be followed by emotional distance, with the child finally estranged, not only from his noncustodial parent, but from his absent siblings as well. This is truly a tragic loss for all concerned.

If the noncustodial parent is able to put his own feelings temporarily aside and look objectively at the child's world, he will be better able to accept the child's decision not to live with him. In the first place, it must be remembered, the child finds himself in a situation not of his own making, forced to make a choice he did not ask to make. Neither Carl nor Frannie, for example, had wanted their parents to divorce, though they were well aware of the tension and unhappiness between their parents. Similarly, neither wanted their mother to move from their home-town to a distant state. Carl and Frannie did not want to be separated from either parent or from each other or from their baby brother. Each made a choice, not to be hurtful or to take sides, but based on personal needs.

Carl and Frannie's parents could have made the same mistake made by many other parents faced with the split-custody situation: They could have retaliated by rejecting the noncustodial child and encouraged their custodial children to do the same. Parents are especially tempted to behave this way if they are very angry with the ex-spouse. Somehow, they feel that by punishing the child, they can further punish the parent. The tragic consequence of this hostile behavior is too often the cessation of all real communication between the noncustodial parent and his child, and between innocent brothers and sisters. This estrangement is made all the more likely when the two ex-spouses and their families are geographically separated.

Fortunately, Carl and Frannie's parents were able, with some effort, to accept their children's decisions regarding custody. Each parent took his noncustodial child out for a "special day," a private time shared only by parent and child. Mrs. Smith took Carl for a ride in the country, and to lunch at his favorite restaurant. There she explained to him, "I know that you love me, and your sister and brother, and you know that we love you very much. But I know how hard it is to move to a new place, and I understand why you want to stay here with your father. Even though I'll be living in another state, I'll write and phone you often. And I want you to visit us in California as often as you can."

Frannie's father took her out for a special day, too, and similarly expressed his feelings. These were difficult and emotional times for both parents and children, but ultimately they served to reassure the children of their parents' love.

In the years that followed, both parents eventually remarried, but they continued to work hard to keep up their relationships with all of their children. There were frequent letters, and photographs and phone calls, and visits during holiday and summer vacations. The parents were especially careful to encourage Carl and Frannie to remain close to each other, and to cultivate the sense that brother and sister, though separated, remained family.

Split-custody situations, then, can stir up particularly powerful feelings of bitterness and rejection in both parents and children. With considerable effort and love, however, even these feelings can be overcome. Otherwise, the child can become doubly a victim, losing not only a parent to feelings of bitterness or rancor, but suffering the loss of his siblings as well.

There is another, relatively new concept in child custody, known as "joint custody." Joint custody gives both parents more or less equal time with their children. There are many variations on the joint-custody theme. A child may spend half a week with one parent and half with the other. Or the time periods may be divided by weeks, or months. Some people are hailing the idea of joint custody as a new answer that solves many of the traditional problems involved in child custody.

Joint custody certainly does have the advantage of ensuring that both parents be actively involved with the child, who thus remains close to both his male and female primary role models. Unfortunately, joint custody poses such enormous practical problems that it can be implemented only under fairly ideal conditions.

We have already seen that the child has a very strong need for a sense of continuity in his life. Very young children, especially, form in infancy a particularly strong attachment to one adult figure: their primary caretaker. They also feel most secure in the physical environment — their own homes — with which they are most familiar. Finally, young children quickly become creatures of habit. They become accustomed to being fed, bathed, and napped at certain specific times of day. When small children are suddenly thrust into a new environment they lose this sense of security. And if a new caretaker suddenly replaces the former familiar caretaker, the child may become very upset. The new caretaker's temperament and his manner — his way of feeding and holding the child — will be different. The child's living habits will be abruptly changed. These constant disruptions would lead to insecurity on the part of an infant or toddler. The small child who is shifted from mother to father on, say, a weekly basis may easily become insecure and unhappy. That child's universe — his home and caretaker — will begin to seem arbitrary and unreliable.

In order better to understand the problems that joint custody may pose for the young child, we should examine how the mind of the child understands the concept of time.

The normal adult has a fairly accurate sense of the passage of time. To be sure, we commonly say that there are periods when the days "seem to fly by," and other periods when "time drags." But we all know how long the experience of an hour, a week, or a year is. We understand what it means to have just "five shopping days left till Christmas," and we know that a close friend will be back with us fairly soon.

The young child, however, simply does not have the experience or the intellectual skills necessary to measure these periods of time accurately. It is no comfort to a two-year-old, for example, to be told that "Mommy will be back home in a week." That child does not, first of all, really understand what a week is. More important, the child experiences time differently from adults. A week is experienced as a very, very long period by a small child; it may seem literally like forever. Only as the child gradually matures does he become able to master a sense of time.

Given the young child's inability to measure and appreciate time accurately, and given his strong need for continuity of place and living habits, joint custody would seem to be more disruptive than beneficial to the young child. Except under extremely favorable circumstances, joint custody probably should not be awarded in cases involving children under age ten. Older children, although they also have a need for order and consistency, are more flexible and, given other arguments for the desirability of joint custody, better able to deal with the lack of continuity. To make joint custody work to the benefit of the child, certain conditions must be set.

For one thing, obviously, joint custody becomes virtually impossible if the parents do not maintain residence in the same town. The child must be able to travel easily from one home to another if she is to divide her days or weeks between homes. Also, there is the problem of the child's schooling. It is quite possible that even parents who live in the same town will reside in different school districts. Parents must then agree on which school the child is to attend and must ensure that the school is accessible to the child from both homes. A long or arduous commute from home to school can tire the child and make her resent the joint-custody situation.

For the child truly to reap the benefits of the joint custody — that is, to feel honestly that she still has two fully involved parents — the child must feel that both her mother's and father's homes are hers, and that she is not merely a guest at one or both of them. It is preferable, if at all possible, for the child to have her own bedroom at both houses. She should also have a sufficient wardrobe and enough familiar objects — books, toys, mementoes — to feel at home. Of course, if the child is used to sharing a bedroom with a sibling, continued sharing with that sibling is not likely to disturb her. However, where one or both parents have remarried and now live with stepchildren, the joint-custody child may be very upset at having to share a bedroom with a new stepsibling. Unless this situation is handled very carefully, the child may come to feel that, instead of having two homes, she is really only an outsider in both her mother's and father's houses.

Finally, all children need a certain consistency in living habits and in moral training. This means that, in joint-custody cases, the father and mother must come to a firm agreement concerning the child's lifestyle and moral tutelage. Parents must agree on what type of responsibilities, limitations, and behavior are to be expected of the child. They must make it absolutely clear to the child what rules and responsibilities she will be held to, and they must present a "united front" to the child on these issues.

To do this, parents must first resolve what may be substantial differences in attitude between themselves and may have to compromise on a number of issues. For example, one parent may think it very important that the older child learn to help cook and serve dinner, while the other parent may prefer to do these things herself. One parent may stress the child's obligation to make her bed and keep her room neat, while the other parent may simply not care.

While these may not be earthshaking issues, it is much easier for the child if the parents can agree on a consistent approach to these everyday problems. Otherwise, the child may use the habits of one parent to undermine the authority of the other ("Daddy never makes me wash the dishes") so that, in the end, the child respects the authority of neither parent. If parents agree to treat the child consistently with regard to her rights and responsibilities, both mother and father will remain, in the child's eyes, the legitimate authority figures she actually wants and needs.

There are other issues, more difficult to resolve, about which parents with joint custody must strive to find a common ground. These involve such things as the child's religious upbringing, education regarding sexual behavior, and discussion of what most people see as moral questions. This "morality" category can cover every subject from pacifism to the use of illicit drugs.

Generally speaking, adolescents are old enough to tolerate the fact that their parents' views may differ on many things. Ideally, by the time of adolescence children will have been educated concerning most aspects of important questions — both the physiological and emotional components of sex, for example — and will be in the process of coming to their own decisions regarding these matters. This does not mean that adolescents no longer have any need of parental guidance, but it does suggest that they are able to accept that adults, including parents, may have very different views on these subjects.

Younger children, however, are more apt to become confused and upset when their parents make an issue out of their disagreement about religious or moral questions. The child's mother, for example, may be devoutly religious, while his father may not believe in God at all. Or the parents may disagree strongly on social issues, or on personal aspects of life, such as sexual habits. This can make life very difficult for the child of joint custody, who is confronted by these conflicting attitudes on a continuing basis. The child who is taken to church and Sunday school one week, only to hear the church ridiculed the next, may have a great deal of difficulty when the time comes for him to form — and act on — his own judgments regarding religion. He may come to view moral questions as problems of loyalty ("Shall I agree with Mom or with Dad?") rather than as important life choices to be resolved independently.

Fortunately, parents who are sensitive to their child's needs can disagree on these and other questions and still enjoy a successful joint-custody experience. This can happen, however, only if the parents agree to disagree; that is, to respect each other's opinion and to make that respect known to the child. On the subject of religion, for example, parents should never ridicule or display contempt for each other's attitudes. Instead, the churchgoing mother might say to her child, "I know that Daddy doesn't believe in God. Some people don't. But I believe that God loves us and takes care of us, and I go to church to thank him in a special way. When you're with me, I want to take you to church, so you can see how people thank God together." Similarly, the nonbelieving father might say, "I don't go to church, but lots of people do. I think it's nice that Mommy takes you with her to her special place." This kind of mutual respect is essential if the child is not to become hopelessly confused and worried about which parent is right, and whether one parent will be punished for being bad or wrong.

The child's need for continuity and consistency in his life places strong demands on the parents to cooperate with each other. It also calls for flexibility on the part of the parents. If the child wants to have an unscheduled dinner with his mother, or spend an extra day or weekend with his father, his parents must be relaxed enough to agree with this. There can be no petty arguments over visitation or other minor issues in the joint-custody situation, and the parents must agree beforehand on such basic issues as the child's schooling. If his parents cannot behave amicably and with respect toward each other, the joint-custody child will find himself literally in the middle of his parents' constant conflict. Since the child must be with both parents, the strain on his loyalty and emotional well-being will be enormous. In cases where the parents cannot cooperate with each other for the good of the child, joint custody should not be allowed.

In the case of the Johnson family, joint custody worked well and made it much easier for the two Johnson children to cope with their parents' divorce. The children — John, twelve, and Gloria, fourteen — lived in a relatively small city in New England. When the Johnsons divorced, it was agreed that Nancy, the wife, would keep the family's three-bedroom home and that the children would continue in the same public junior high and high schools. George Johnson, the father, took a large apartment in another neighborhood, easily accessible by public transportation. The divorce was amicable, and the parents agreed on joint custody, with the children spending two weeks a month with their mother and two with their father. During "off" weeks John and Gloria would frequently talk with their absent parent by telephone, and would visit that parent for dinner once or twice.

The parents spoke with each other, by telephone at least, once a week to keep each other informed about the children's activities, progress in school, health, and other matters. They also agreed to observe the same rules regarding the children's curfews and social activities. Thus, they were able to keep track of the children and resolve potential problems before they got out of hand.

This was particularly important in the case of twelve-year-old John, who began to act out his resentment when his mother started dating shortly after the divorce. John attempted to play one parent off against the other by telling his father that he was visiting his mother (and vice versa) when he was really spending his evenings with a group of young people who were experimenting with alcohol. Several of these boys, at the ages of twelve and thirteen, already had serious drinking problems. Since one or both of the Johnson children often spontaneously decided to spend a night with their "off-week" parent, neither John's mother nor father immediately sensed anything odd about their son's nights out. But soon enough, in the course of their regular telephone conversations, John's mysterious behavior became known. This enabled his parents jointly to seek professional counseling for John, before his drinking became a dangerous habit.

In the joint-custody situation, relatively affluent parents are at an advantage. Not every divorced couple can afford to keep two separate homes, each large enough to have extra bedrooms for their children. Often, in fact, the income of at least one party to a divorce is seriously depleted by the divorce, and that party must seek out cheaper living quarters and a more modest lifestyle.

Certain divorced couples have solved this problem by keeping one family home and one smaller apartment. In this arrangement, instead of having the children travel from one parent's house to the other's, the parents do the traveling. Thus, the mother might spend two weeks of every other month, or perhaps one month of every two, with her children in the family home. Then she would move to smaller quarters, while the father moved into the family home for his custodial period.

This arrangement may have the advantage of making the children, especially younger children, feel more secure. Instead of shifting from one house to another they have one house, one bedroom, one neighborhood, one home base. It does, however, present problems for the parents, who must be willing to uproot themselves constantly and move from one quarter to another. This presents practical problems for most adults. It certainly, among other things, creates difficulties for the divorced parent who wishes to remarry, since he can hardly expect his new spouse to deny herself a permanent household in order to spend more time with children who are not her own. Of course, should the new spouse bring children of her own into the marriage, the one-home approach becomes impossible.

Though joint custody may theoretically be the best solution to the custody problem, it is practical only if a number of preconditions exist. For one thing, there must be a great deal of cooperation — *amicable* cooperation — between the parents. Grudging cooperation with overtones of bitterness or rancor is simply not good enough. In cases where the divorced couple is still emotionally at war, joint custody can do more harm than good, since the children will be constantly exposed to their parents' bitter exchanges. Moreover, in such situations, questions of loyalty ("Who treats you better, your mother or me?") will constantly be held over the child's head.

Other factors, such as the child's age, and such practical factors as geography and finances — must also be considered in determining whether joint custody is an appropriate option in a given situation.

Thus, although joint custody may well be the wave of the fu-

ture, at present sole custody is still the rule. It also remains largely true, at least for the present, that the child's mother will gain
sole custody. In sole-custody situations, the question of the noncustodial parent's visitation rights assumes primary importance.
It is through these visits that the noncustodial parent retains
his emotional ties to his child. Considering this, it is unfortunate, indeed tragic, that so many parents use the question of
visitation rights as still another battlefield on which to join arms.
The most common, which we discussed before, is to deny the
father visitation rights when he fails to make his court-ordered
child-support or alimony payment. This is a very difficult area.
Although one can argue that this denial is an eminently justi-
fiable act, and the only weapon the ex-wife has to force her husband to resume payment, I have to repeat that the mother must
put her own feelings aside and allow her children to see their
father. Otherwise, she falls into the trap of using her children as
a weapon. Besides — and this is an important point — some experts feel that a father who keeps in touch with his children is
more likely to realize their financial needs and to resume his
child-support payments.

Even when the father is allowed to see his children, however,
there are many destructive emotional games that bitter ex-spouses
engage in. The father who knows that his ex-wife has made plans
of her own for the visitation hours, which may be her only free
time, may deliberately and consistently show up late for the visits. In so doing, he may have gained some pleasure by spoiling
his ex-wife's plans. But he has also demonstrated to his children,
who were looking forward to the visit, that he is undependable
and even that he doesn't love them enough to want to see them.
After all, why else wouldn't he bother to be on time, when they
were so patiently waiting for him?

Six-year-old Michael was a victim of his parents' ongoing battles. Michael's father, according to the divorce agreement, was

to see him every Saturday, from 10:00 A.M. to 7:00 P.M. Invariably, the father would promise his son that he would take him to a ball game, or for a picnic out in the countryside. But, more often than not, the boy would be dressed and waiting for his father from early morning until midafternoon, when the father would either show up late or phone to say that he couldn't visit because "something had come up." The father's real aim, though he barely realized it on a conscious level, was to get at Michael's mother, who would have made her own plans for the day and invariably had to cancel them. Michael's mother retaliated, from time to time, by refusing for periods of a month or so to allow the father to see Michael at all. Michael, of course, did not understand this elaborate parental game: He suffered instead the anger and self-hatred of the child who knows he is not valued by his parent.

Susan, aged eight, was similarly victimized by her parents' behavior, though their interaction was more subtle. For example, when Susan's father arrived one Saturday to take his daughter to an important family wedding, he found that her mother had dressed her in old blue jeans and sneakers because "Susan would rather go to the park." By the time the child had dressed properly, she and her father were late for the wedding. At the wedding reception, Susan was extremely ill at ease, knowing she had been the cause of her parents' argument. This nervousness, plus a combination of rich foods given the girl at the reception, caused Susan to be sick when she reached home. This provided the occasion for another argument, in which the mother accused Susan's father of being "irresponsible" and "abusive" to his daughter. Here again, Susan was the emotional — and even the physical — loser.

As a mature, caring parent, it is important to accept the fact that your children need both parents as role models and for love and support. Even if you and your spouse justly hate each other, you must see to it that parental visitation is not used as an occasion to injure each other, but is planned and carried out with a minimum of conflict and with the child's welfare in mind. The custodial parent must have the child ready for the visiting parent, and the visiting parent must be careful to arrive regularly and at the scheduled time. Of course, both parents must allow for some flexibility on the visitation schedule.

Inevitably, there will be occasions when it is highly inconvenient or practically impossible for the visiting parent to keep his appointment with the child. At such times, if at all possible, the visiting parent should let the child know *well in advance* that he will be unable to be there, and he should explain why. Nothing is sadder than a small child left literally waiting on the doorstep for a parent who never arrives.

There may also be occasions when the scheduled visit time is inconvenient for the child. The child may be reluctant to go out with Dad on Saturday afternoons if his Little League baseball games are scheduled for those afternoons.

Caring parents will recognize the practical realities of such situations and will allow for flexibility in the visiting schedule. Forcing parents and child to stick to the letter of the divorce agreement may serve to punish one or both parents, but it may also arouse resentment and insecurity in the child. The child should be able to feel that he has real emotional and physical access to the noncustodial parent. If the child wants to sleep over at the noncustodial parent's house for an extra night or make an occasional unscheduled visit, both parents should attempt to accommodate him.

Something should be said here about the *quality* of the child's visit with his nonresident parent. Very often, the parent who only gets to visit his child weekly, or even less often, feels guilty about his absence from the child's daily life. For this and other reasons, the noncustodial parent more often than not feels that he must make his visiting hours special by formally entertaining the child. Thus, the parent's visiting day is always used to take the child to a movie, or to the circus, or to an amusement park. The visiting parent never appears without a gift for the child, and he may allow the child to gorge on junk foods that are forbidden at home.

The visiting parent may feel that these special treats will compensate the child for time missed with the parent, and ensure the child's love. Actually, if visits are always filled with special activities, both parents — and the child — may suffer. The custodial parent, of course, may be placed in the role of strict and unreasonable tyrant: "Daddy always lets me have cookies before dinner. Why don't you?" But the visiting parent also suffers. By filling his own time with his child with artificial, formal activities, he and the child may lose the opportunity to really get to know each other.

Some visits, at least, would be better if they were planned around normal daily activities: playing at the visiting parent's home, helping him make dinner, going for a walk, or just talking. This way, parent and child will get to know each other better. The child will ultimately feel more comfortable with the visiting parent and will see him as a real person rather than as some unnatural Santa Claus figure, always laden with gifts.

But whatever the custody and visitation arrangements, the child's life will definitely be changed by divorce. In the next chapter, we'll look at some forms that the child's reaction may take.

5

The Child's Reaction
to Divorce

INEVITABLY, all caring parents worry about the effects their divorce will have on their children. They have heard, as we all have, tragic stories of "problem children" from "broken homes." Many commonly blame the broken home for such juvenile problems as alcohol or drug abuse. Serious juvenile crimes — theft or acts of violence, for example — are also seen sometimes as stemming from the failure of the broken or single-parent home.

Naturally, with this in mind, many divorced parents are quick to panic when their children show symptoms of what the parents believe are psychological or behavioral disturbances. Parents may overreact to what they see as signs of future juvenile delinquency or mental illness in their child.

I would ask you to remember two things. First, the child of divorce — even the healthiest child — will inevitably react in some way to the divorce experience. Not infrequently, these reactions may seem strange, difficult to understand. The child's behavior may sometimes appear odd, or hostile, or even bizarre. This behavior usually means that the child is using his own set of emotional tools to work through, and eventually accept, his experience of the divorce. In this chapter we will describe these tools, and discuss how you can best help your child through this difficult period.

Second, I must ask you to reject the clichéd notion that divorce necessarily brings on neurotic, deranged, or even criminal behavior in the child's later life. Remember the studies discussed in chapter 2 of this book that strongly indicate it is not merely the absence of a parent but rather psychological and/or physical abuse or neglect that tend to harm the child. It is the aim of this book, and the aim of every caring parent, to avoid unconsciously inflicting psychological harm on the child during divorce. I am confident that loving parents who put their children's interests first can help them to make a healthy adjustment to their new life situation.

Every child will inevitably experience one or more emotional reactions to his parents' divorce. However, because we are dealing with children, who cannot accurately explain their own complicated feelings, these reactions may be disguised. That is, a child's behavior may not always mean what it seems to mean. The young girl in chapter 1 who reacted to her parents' divorce by appearing to be entirely uninterested and untroubled was neither selfish nor unfeeling. Rather, her behavior said, "I cannot deal with or accept this painful situation right now. I will try to ignore it for the time being, and seek the comfort and support of my friends."

The little boy who asks only such apparently trivial questions as "Will Daddy still take me to the zoo?" after a divorce is expressing similar feelings. He is really asking, "What will happen to me now? Will you and Daddy desert me? Who will take care of me?" The child is actually expressing his fears, and his grief, not merely his fondness for the zoo.

Because the child's true feelings are so often disguised, the parent should be alert for signs of *any* general behavioral change in the child. Any behavior that seems uncharacteristic may signal the child's struggle to understand his changed life.

It is also important to understand that these changes in behavior may occur at virtually any time in the period immediately before, during, or after the divorce. It takes some children longer than others to realize the full implications of their parents' separation. Some children may have a delayed reaction to the divorce, coming several months after the event. A common first response of the young child, who cannot understand the legal implications of divorce, is confusion. Because egocentricity is so strong in the young child, such a child is more apt than his elder siblings to blame himself for the divorce. Older children, more sophisticated and knowledgeable about the nature of divorce, may tend to reveal their feelings in other ways. Each child will react to the divorce situation in an individual way, depending on his personality, age, and emotional and intellectual development.

A child's emotional reaction to divorce, when it comes, may take a number of forms. The most important, and common, of these are known as *denial, depression, grief, anger, regression,* and *acting out.* These states are what psychiatrists and psychologists call defense mechanisms. A defense mechanism is simply a way in which the child — or person of any age, for that matter — makes bearable some overwhelming anxiety, grief, or other painful emotional state. In other words, the child instinctively adopts a certain form of behavior that fights off or neutralizes a reality that, if fully acknowledged, would cause him to experience overpowering psychological pain. All of us have used defense mechanisms at one time or another to allow us temporarily to put off emotional pain until we feel strong enough to deal with the underlying truth that caused us that pain.

We can best examine how defense mechanisms work by looking at *denial,* which is frequently used by children of divorcing parents, most especially by the younger child.

Denial means exactly what the word implies: the refusal to believe an unpleasant reality long after that reality has become obvious to any objective observer. There are many ways in which a child may articulate his denial of the fact of his parents' divorce. Take the case of Charles, a six-year-old boy whose parents received their final divorce decree. Charles's father had moved out of the family home several months before, after both parents had carefully explained to the boy the details — and the permanence — of their separation.

Charles was greatly affected by his parents' separation. He was deeply attached to both of his parents, and this radical change in his life threatened the boy with powerful fears: fear of separation from his father, fear of abandonment by his mother, and fear that his parents' divorce might open the way for other unpleasant changes in his life. If engulfed by these fears all at once, Charles could have panicked, completely overwhelmed. Instead, the child instinctively protected himself by refusing to believe the obvious: that his parents were indeed separated.

At first, Charles told everyone — relatives, teachers, schoolmates — that his father was "away at a meeting" and that he would return any day. He carefully brought in the evening newspaper every day and placed it on the table near his father's favorite chair, "so Daddy can read it when he gets home." He saved all of his written homework assignments and school tests, "so Daddy can see them when he comes home." And he became quite hysterical when his mother tried to turn her ex-husband's den into a guest room. "Where will Daddy work if he doesn't have his den?" the boy asked tearfully.

Charles's mother was at first annoyed, and then alarmed, by her son's behavior. She could not understand why her son continued to "lie" to his friends about the divorce. She began to feel that her son might be mentally ill, might even be having hallucinations in which he "saw" his absent father. Though she tried to talk sense to the boy, Charles remained firm: "No, you're wrong," he repeated firmly. "Daddy's coming home. I know it!"

If Charles's mother had consulted a psychologist, she would have discovered that Charles's use of denial, in this instance, did not mean that he was disturbed or mentally ill. All normal children — and adults — occasionally use denial to help them gradually accept some unpleasant or painful reality, as Charles eventually did.

Occasionally, a person will find himself or herself unable to make a healthy adjustment to a painful reality. In such a case, denial may be used in an exaggerated, unhealthy way, long after it is appropriate, so that, instead of helping the person gradually to adjust to a new reality, it interferes with a healthy adjustment to a new life situation. How can a parent know when his child has reached the point where his denial of the divorce has become harmful? There are basically two questions the parent should ask. The first is: "Am I giving my child enough time to adjust to these vital changes in his life?" The second — and perhaps the critical — question is, "Is my child's refusal to admit the reality of our divorce interfering with his ability to function normally and to enjoy life?"

To answer the first question we must ask another question: What is a "normal" period of adjustment for your child? This will vary considerably according to the child's age and emotional and physical development, as well as the circumstances of the divorce. Generally speaking, though, you should be able to detect certain changes in the child's use of denial over a period of some months. This does not mean that six-year-old Charles, for example, will suddenly realize the truth about the divorce and stop claiming that "Daddy's coming home." The changes in Charles are apt to be more gradual and subtle. Charles may continue to say, "Daddy's coming home," but begin to say it in a less emphatic, more questioning tone. Or he may, one day, unexpectedly say to a friend, "Maybe Daddy isn't coming home."

He might say nothing, but merely stop laying out his father's evening newspaper, or arguing about the fate of the room that had been his father's den.

All of these small signals are signs that Charles is coming, within himself, to accept the truth. In this case, Charles's mother was wise not to argue with the boy, not to force him to face the facts before Charles was ready. Instead, Charles chose his own moment to accept reality, when he felt strongest and ready to cope.

But what if the months had dragged on, with Charles showing no sign of relinquishing his fantasy that "Daddy is coming back"? The questions that must be asked, then, are: "Is this becoming an obsession with Charles? Is it interfering with his ability to perform his schoolwork, to make and keep friends, to relate to his family? Or is it adversely affecting his overall social and emotional development?"

By observing your child's behavior, you should be able to find relatively concrete answers to these questions. For example, in Charles's case, does he go out and play with his friends, or insist on staying at home in case "Daddy comes home"? Does he get anxious when his mother leaves the house, for fear that "Daddy will be mad when he comes home and you're not here"? Does he refuse to go to school because he wants to be there when "Daddy comes home"?

If, after an extended period, the child's denial of divorce is still absolute, and if it interferes with his relationships at home and with his peers and with his ability to function at school, the child will benefit from professional counseling. But if his one form of unusual behavior — his denial of the divorce — is not otherwise affecting his ability to function in the home or in school, it may be wise to allow him more time to work things out on his own. The parent can help, in this case, by waiting for the child to bring up this painful subject when he is ready. Thus, when, after several months, the child offers a tentative "Daddy's not coming home, is he?" the parent should respond calmly and matter-of-factly, "That's right, Charles. Daddy's not going to live here with us anymore. But he still loves you very much, and will visit as often as he can."

As we have noted, denial is one defense mechanism that can be used by persons of any age. Generally, however, it tends to be seen in its exaggerated forms most frequently in smaller children. Denial becomes somewhat less as the child grows older, though it may continue to form a part of a person's behavioral repertoire throughout life.

It is not too difficult for a parent to know when his child is denying reality. But the child may have other emotional reactions to divorce which are much less straightforward in appearance and more difficult to deal with. Two such reactions are *grief* and *depression*.

It is important here that we make a distinction between depression and grief. *Grief* is a normal reaction to the loss of an important person or object. We all experience grief at certain times in the course of our lives. Inevitably, certain loved friends and relatives will die, or leave us permanently. Love affairs and marriages may end unhappily. We may have to part with certain objects or properties that hold special emotional significance for us. In fact, it may well be that the person who goes through life without experiencing grief wouldn't ever have the critical capacity to give and receive love.

The end of a marriage certainly represents a significant loss for both parents and children. Grief is certainly a normal reaction to divorce; no matter how unpleasant the later married life of a couple might have been, the finality of divorce is bound to remind the newly separated ex-spouses of the hope, happiness, and love with which they originally entered their marriage. In a very real emotional sense, many divorcing spouses, even those who appear to react calmly and intellectually to the divorce process, feel on some level that the divorce represents a major failure in their personal lives.

Thus it is to be expected that the ex-spouse will grieve — will, in fact, enter a period of mourning — after the divorce. We are all familiar with the most common manifestations of grief: tearfulness, crying, sadness, a temporary obsession with and nostalgia for the past, and such things as temporary disruption of eating and sleeping habits.

Many people must go through the grieving process in order to put the past truly behind them and begin to construct new and satisfying lives. But children, too, will usually grieve over their parents' separation and divorce. After all, they are experiencing a very great loss: the loss of an intact family. How can the parent best help his child through this painful period?

The normal grieving process is self-limiting; that is, it will become less intense with time. The grieving child may thus go through a mourning period in which he is tearful, overly dependent, and without interest in school or play. He may also suffer temporary disruption of eating and sleeping habits.

One other rather dramatic manifestation of grief should be mentioned here. It has often been observed in cases involving the loss — through death or absence — of a loved one, that the person "left behind" will unconsciously begin to imitate the person "lost." For example, an elderly, rather timid lady had lived for nearly fifty years with a somewhat overbearing, highly opinionated husband. In the months following her husband's death, her friends began to notice a pronounced change in the widow's manner. She changed from being a very shy, laconic woman to a rather assertive person with very pronounced opinions. In fact, she had unconsciously adopted the manner of her dead husband. This frequently happens to people who grieve deeply for a loved one. Subconsciously, they try to bring the dead person back to life, by taking on his mannerisms and personality.

The child of divorce may do something very similar. Eight-year-old Kenny, in the weeks following his father's departure from the family home, began to take on several new behavioral traits. He became extremely solicitous about his mother, performing the household tasks — taking out the garbage, walking the dog — that his father had always done. He changed from a rather fragile, openly sensitive little boy to the strong, silent type that his father had been, fiercely repressing any display of emotion. This little eight-year-old even made a great display of poring over the evening paper, as his father had done, and insisting on watching the TV evening news!

It was obvious that Kenny, missing his father deeply, was trying to keep a part of his father's personality with him. Unfortunately, this method of imitating the traits of dead or absent loved ones could have led, in Kenny's case, to further problems. For one thing, the more the little boy acted like "the man of the house," the more likely his mother would be to regard him as such. And we have already seen the guilt and distress that a little boy feels when he believes that he has beaten out his father for his mother's attention. No matter how much such a boy might secretly dream of being the sole focus of his mother's love, he simply cannot cope with the guilty feelings that he will have if he is treated as a substitute husband.

Kenny's behavior could cause other complications, as well. It is entirely possible that, when Kenny began to act so much like his father, Kenny's mother might have subconsciously been reminded of the negative, hurtful emotions she felt for her former husband. Unwittingly, she could react to her son with hostility simply because he reminded her so much of his father! Situations like this can lead to emotional chaos, since neither mother nor child fully understands her own, or the other's, behavior. Often, in these situations, professional counseling is needed to unravel the emotional tangle that results.

Depression differs from grief, which is, as has been stated earlier, a normal, essentially healthy, process, and one that should help the child resolve the divorce experience. Depression, like grief, may be self-limiting and self-resolving, or it may continue to the point where it interferes grossly with the child's life.

What is depression? How is it manifest, and how can the parent help his depressed child?

At the start, it must be stated that depression in children is not yet well understood. Indeed, years ago there was a widely held view that children, especially younger children, simply lacked the fully developed psychological qualities that played a part in depression. Today, it is generally accepted that even very small children are capable of suffering serious depression. In fact, there are reports of children as young as age five who have been depressed enough actually to attempt suicide. Unfortunately, in children as well as in adults, depression may mask itself in a variety of symptoms, including behavioral changes and physical illness.

Depression can be difficult to diagnose in children. We all either have experienced depression in ourselves, as adults, or have seen the signs of it in someone close to us. Indeed, some statistics would indicate that one out of every four American adults will suffer a significant period of depression at some point in his life. Some of the symptoms of this very common disorder are: insomnia, sudden weight gain or loss, periods of weeping for no apparent reason, feelings of hopelessness, loss of self-esteem, and a sense that things will never get any better. Severely depressed people may find it difficult to concentrate on work or study and may shun the company of others, preferring quiet and solitude.

Depression usually follows a loss of some kind — the loss of a loved one through death, loss of a job or lover, or some financial or other loss that affects the person's sense of self-esteem.

Oddly enough, it seems that depression following the death or departure of a person for whom we have mixed feelings is more intense and apt to last longer than depression following the loss of someone under less complicated circumstances. That is, if a person has feelings of both love and anger toward another person, he is apt to be more depressed by the loss of that person. This may sound strange until we realize that depression is, at least partly, "anger turned inward," that is, anger and guilt directed at the self. The more guilty we feel about our relationship with the lost one, the more angry at ourselves — the more depressed — we tend to become.

In children, it is often difficult to distinguish between the symptoms of depression and the symptoms displayed in the normal grieving process. Generally speaking, depression and grief differ from each other mainly in duration. Grief dissipates with time; depression often lingers on and begins to interfere in a very basic way with the child's ability to learn, to work, to play, to make friends — in short, to lead a normal life.

We have already listed some of the symptoms of depression as they are experienced by adults: disturbances in eating and sleeping, feelings of worthlessness and self-hatred, feelings of hopelessness about the future. In addition, however, it seems that the depressed child can present a variety of other depressive symptoms not ordinarily found in adults. In fact, one expert has stated that depression in children can take on a chameleonlike quality, with many behavioral manifestations.

Where does that leave us? First of all, we have already seen that depression is more likely to occur in persons who have experienced mixed feelings of love and anger toward the "lost" (i.e., divorced) parents. Thus, it is quite possible that the child of divorce is more likely to become depressed if the divorce has been a highly emotional one that has aroused in him feelings of sorrow, anger, and even hatred. It will commonly be harder for such a child to resolve the divorce experience without difficulty.

The depressed child may show emotional distress in a variety of ways, from insomnia to bed-wetting to declining performance in school. For the parent, however, the important thing is not to find a proper label for the child's emotional state but to assess the degree to which that emotional state threatens to interfere with the child's permanent development.

Take the case of two sisters: Alice, eight, and Cindy, ten. Both children had been given into their father's custody after the divorce, with the consent of their mother, who had taken a demanding job in a distant city. Both girls loved their father, and he was fortunate enough to work out of his home, so that, together with a full-time housekeeper, he was able to give them ample time and attention.

Despite their father's best intentions, both girls, naturally enough, missed the presence and affection of their mother. And they displayed their grief in similar ways: by crying, loss of interest in school and play, and frequent nightmares. As the weeks wore on, however, their father noticed a difference between the behavior of the two sisters.

Alice, the younger, gradually began to regain her enthusiasm for school and her eagerness to play with her friends. After a period of clinging to her father, she became more independent, even asking for permission to sleep over at the home of her closest friend. Her nightmares became less frequent after several weeks, and she ordinarily slept through the night.

Ten-year-old Cindy, on the other hand, became less and less able to cope with daily life. The spells of weeping and tearfulness continued. Her problems with school increased, to the point where she began to refuse to leave the house altogether, clinging to her father and presenting various excuses for her reluctance to go to school. This behavior, known as "school refusal," is common among children of recently divorced parents and may present serious problems.

School refusal often occurs as a result of the child's fear of desertion. That is, the child who has experienced the departure of one parent from the family may, in some cases, become extremely insecure about the love and devotion of the remaining custodial parent. She may become so frightened by the possibility of parental desertion that she will work herself into near-hysteria if the custodial parent even leaves her with a baby sitter for a few hours. Similarly, such children commonly fear that, if they leave the house to go to school, their remaining parent may "disappear" before they return. To be sure, in other cases school refusal may stem from factors relating to learning disabilities or to serious problems in the child's peer relationships. Little Cindy, however, had no such learning problems. Before her parents' divorce, in fact, her teachers had evaluated her as "an exceptionally able and interested student." But in the months following her mother's departure, Cindy's grades plummeted. She also became uncharacteristically shy, avoiding her former friends and refusing to take part in those social occasions, such as birthday parties, that she had previously enjoyed.

At first, Cindy's father did not recognize her school refusal for what it was. This was understandable, since the problem is often disguised as a series of "mysterious" physical illnesses. Like most children, she did not merely state, "I'm afraid to go to school." Indeed, she woke up each school morning with a physical ailment. "My head hurts," Cindy would complain, lying listlessly in bed. Or, "My stomach hurts. I think I'm going to throw up." At this point, Cindy's concerned father would ordinarily allow her to stay home from school. As his daughter's "illnesses" dragged on, he became increasingly worried, taking the child to a succession of pediatricians, one of whom finally, after examining the girl, explained the "school-refusal" syndrome to her father.

This case provides one illustration of the difference between the normal grieving process and a more prolonged case of depression. Cindy's sister, Alice, certainly *grieved* over the absence of her mother, and this grief temporarily affected her day-to-day functioning at home and in school. But Alice resolved the grieving process naturally, while Cindy fell into a serious depression.

In Cindy's case, her father and the pediatrician agreed that the girl needed professional counseling. With therapy, Cindy's school refusal and other symptoms of depression gradually disappeared. If school refusal is the only manifestation of the child's depression, a sensitive and knowledgeable parent may be able to help alleviate the problem without professional help.

For example, the school-refusal child will commonly complain of physical ailments on school mornings, but rarely on weekends and holidays. Also, if the child is allowed to stay home on school days, his symptoms will usually improve radically by midmorning. Of course, the parent should always be careful to take the child's temperature and watch carefully to see if the child vomits or displays other objective signs of illness. Also, if the child's complaints persist, a trip to the child's doctor is probably in order. But if, after taking these precautions, the parent is convinced that the child is persistently faking illness, the parent must begin to intervene. To allow the child to continue to stay home from school on a pretext will only encourage his fears and disrupt his school adjustment.

Here you, the parent, should be firm, but not angry. You should attempt to minimize the child's symptoms, by saying: "I'm sorry that your head hurts, but you'll feel better once you've had breakfast and gotten on the school bus." You must also be careful to reassure the child that you will not "disappear" if the child goes off to school. In some cases, it is helpful if you can, at least at first, physically accompany the child to school and be waiting for him outside the school in the afternoon.

Depression, with its varied symptoms, may be difficult to identify. A child may have other responses to the divorce situation that are easier to recognize, though also difficult for the parent to deal with. Some of these common responses are *anger*, *acting out*, and *regression*.

We have all experienced *anger*. The child of divorce, however, who often feels angry over the breakup of his home, sometimes displays this anger in ways that adults find hard to understand. It is characteristic of children, especially very small children, that they do not know enough to direct their anger toward the appropriate target. The small child who trips and falls over a toy will often blame his accident and hurt on the first person he sees. Small children are often not sophisticated enough, either intellectually or emotionally, to fully understand the situations that made them angry in the first place. They cannot identify the real culprit. Divorce thus leaves them angry and confused, as well as unhappy.

Sometimes, therefore, children will blame the noncustodial parent for the divorce, regardless of the objective facts. Just as often, they will vent their anger at the parent who presents the most visible target — the custodial parent. In most cases, this period of anger is a natural reaction that the child will have to work through. Parents should realize this and try not to be overly hurt or upset by their child's displays of anger. Remember, your child is really angry at the divorce *situation*, not at any one person. His anger will subside as his understanding grows.

This most emphatically does *not* mean that you should allow yourself to become the child's target of abuse. But you should keep in mind that, if you overreact to the child's displays of temper, the child will only be encouraged to continue those displays.

Remember a basic principle from our earlier discussion: Above all else, a child craves attention. Even negative, painful attention will do. Strange as it may seem, a child would rather be verbally or even physically abused by his parents than be ignored by them. We have all seen children who continued to engage in forbidden behavior in full view of their parents, as if taunting the parents to respond. Children have a truly pathetic need to be noticed, no matter what the consequences.

The angry child is likely to direct her anger at one or the other of her divorced parents. Often the child will be quicker to display anger at the parent with whom she feels more secure. Little Jane is likely to have temper tantrums directed at her mother only if she feels fairly safe in assuming that the mother will not desert her. In fact, these tantrums may well be a sort of test of her mother's loyalty: Does she really love her enough to put up even with her anger?

In such a situation the parent may well feel doubly abused because of her conviction that the child's anger is unjust. The young mother who has suddenly been deserted by her husband, with no means of support, will find it especially difficult to be tolerant if her children direct their own anger over the separation at her. And it is extremely difficult not to take things personally when your own child is standing in the middle of your living room, shouting, "I hate you, Mommy." At such time parents may understandably be tempted to throw away all expert advice, this book included.

But it is important here to understand the concept that psychiatrists call *acting out*. This term once had a very particular psychoanalytical meaning. But today acting out, as used by psy-

chiatrists and psychologists, refers to almost any form of deliber-
ate misconduct on the part of a patient. Smaller children may be
said to be acting out if they consistently break rules laid down by
their parents, get into fights and engage in delinquent conduct
with their peers, or bully other children. In older children and
adolescents, the behavior involved in acting out may have more
serious social consequences, sometimes involving acts of juvenile
delinquency, sexual promiscuity, or use of alcohol or other drugs.

It is often difficult to see behind the veneer of the hostile, distant child or adolescent. Yet it is true that the child who acts
out is doing so in a twisted attempt to let others know of his anger, his fears and insecurities, and his overwhelming need to be
loved. This period may be the most exasperating and troublesome for both parent and child. What is the conscientious parent to do with and for the child who is acting out?

I think that there are two different types of situations involved
here, and they call for two different types of response. The first,
and more dramatic, occurs when the child engages in behavior
that is clearly dangerous and self-destructive. The most common
of these situations involves the child's or adolescent's involvement with alcohol or drugs. Unfortunately, our current social
reality includes the unhappy fact that both alcohol and drugs
(or *other* drugs, I should say, since alcohol itself is a drug) are
relatively easy for our children to obtain. I have seen children
as young as seven years old who have already developed serious
drinking problems.

Psychiatric theory holds (and I firmly believe) that most
people who abuse alcohol or other drugs do so because of deep-
seated emotional needs — in other words, that they are acting
out inner conflicts or feelings. Theoretically, in an ideal situation, such children could benefit from intensive long-term psychotherapy. In real life, of course, alcoholism and drug abuse,
while they may be only symptoms of inner conflict, are also in-

dependent problems that can harm and even kill young people. The crucial thing, here, is to help the child to conquer the so-called symptom, and worry about the psychoanalytic implications later.

I cannot overestimate the harm that alcohol and other drug abuse can do to the child or adolescent. Abuse of drugs or alcohol on the part of your child calls for the immediate involvement of professional help. There are now excellent hospital and outpatient clinics, as well as private practitioners, who do excellent work with youngsters who have a problem with drugs or alcohol. For those with a drinking problem, I also suggest the involvement of Alcoholics Anonymous. This well-respected self-help group, which costs nothing and preserves the anonymity of its members, has chapters in virtually every city. Its offshoots, Alateen and Al-Anon, help teen-agers and the families of alcoholics, respectively, to learn how best to deal with the alcoholic family member.

I must emphasize: If you have reason to believe that your child is involved with drugs or alcohol, seek professional advice immediately. If you do not have access to a reputable psychiatrist or social-service agency, you should feel free to call a clergyman (even if you are not a church member) or your local hospital social-service department for referral to a specially trained counselor or facility. Other types of acting out that have serious social consequences are repeated truancy, vandalism, and other acts of juvenile delinquency. Obviously, even as attention-getting devices these are serious matters.

There are many more examples of acting out, however, especially in younger children, that are considerably more irritating to the parent than they are illegal or truly harmful to the child. We are all familiar with these. Commonly, in the younger child these take the form of deliberately disobeying rules, frequent temper tantrums at home or at school, and inability to get along with peers. Such a child, for example, might suddenly become the class clown or even the class bully in an effort to express his frustration.

In older children, acting out may also take the form of truancy, frequent fights, consistent disregard of parental curfews, and verbal abuse of parents.

These episodes can be both exasperating and exhausting to the beleaguered parent. In fact, the parent's instinctive and immediate response may quite naturally be to fight fire with fire — to shout back when the child shouts, to respond with yet another punishment when the child refuses to clean his room. All of these emotional responses, while entirely understandable, are sure to show the child that he has succeeded in getting to you.

What is the parent to do? After all, the child who is behaving badly in public, or verbally abusing his mother or father at home, or torturing his classmates, obviously must be shown that such behavior is entirely unacceptable. Yet here I am, in effect, telling the parent not to get excited.

Remember the basic fact that I have referred to several times previously — a child will do nearly anything to attract attention, even negative attention. The child behaves badly, at least in part, to get the satisfaction of his parent's attention. The more exercised and emotional the parent gets, the more satisfaction the child feels. This is *not* because the child is inherently nasty or mean-tempered. It simply means that the child, having just been through the divorce process, is feeling insecure about his parent's love. His unattractive behavior is a sort of test for the parent — the child wants to be assured that, even if he behaves badly, the parent will still love him. In a strange way, a parent's outburst or tirade, or even a spanking, can serve to reassure the child that his parent still cares for him.

But this way of thinking on the child's part must be corrected. Otherwise, this sad and unhealthy habit of searching for negative attention as proof of love will follow the child through later life. The adult who is always picking quarrels with his spouse or who is constantly seeking sympathy for imaginary aches and pains is often one who, as a child, learned to attract this sort of negative attention and to look on it as the only form of love. Needless to say, this kind of behavior eventually wears other people out. Relationships based on negative attention tend to be neurotic and short-lived. In order to be fully capable of experiencing and enjoying love, the child must learn that love is based on positive qualities, such as shared experiences, the meeting of mutual needs, and honest, open affection.

The parent, then, must not inadvertently encourage — psychologists use the term *reinforce* — the child's acting-out behavior. Ideally, the behavior, if not extreme, should be ignored. Take a very common example, that of temper tantrums in young children. If your five-year-old daughter, for instance, throws screaming, thrashing tantrums in your home, you should try simply not responding to them. Similarly, if the girl has tantrums in public places, such as department stores, the parent should *never* scream at or, above all, strike her. Instead, the parent should immediately and firmly remove the child from the public place. Once home, the child should be informed that she will not be taken out again unless her behavior improves. Again, the parent should try to relay this information without becoming emotional or excited himself.

If acting-out behavior, such as tantrums, can be ignored, it is very likely to disappear by itself. Granted, ignoring a screaming child may demand a parent with nerves of steel. Even when the behavior cannot be ignored, however, the parent can adopt another helpful tactic. Rather than fall back on the instinctive angry impulse to punish the child, the parent might try to distract the child with more positive activities. This, of course, works most successfully with smaller children. If four-year-old Laura is about to start decorating the living room walls with her finger-paints, you might enthusiastically produce a pad of paper, and ask Laura to draw a "special picture" on the pad. Or you might try to draw the child's attention to another project altogether. The *worst* thing you can do (and, unfortunately, an entirely natural reaction) is to scream at Laura, heatedly lecture her on the subject of painting on walls, or even strike her. This type of emotional response will only teach Laura that one sure-fire way to get your attention is to paint on the walls.

A parent's emotional overreaction to his child's misbehavior, then, will only encourage an insecure child to continue to misbehave. But there are other, more positive steps you can take to help your child through a difficult acting-out phase.

As we have explained, the child who reacts to his parents' divorce with a sudden spate of rule-breaking or other troublesome behavior has been emotionally shaken by the divorce and is seeking proof of his parents' love. Therefore, you must help your child to understand that it is positive, constructive behavior that fosters and strengthens love and not reward your child's negative behavior by overreacting to it. But you *should* reward the child's constructive behavior with praise, attention, and affection. Take the example of four-year-old Laura and her finger-paints. Laura's mother was right in preventing the child from defacing the walls. Instead of becoming emotional, she wisely gave Laura the pad on which to paint a special picture. When Laura later presented her mother with the finished painting, Laura's mother praised it, hugged the child, and prominently displayed the painting on the family bulletin board in the kitchen.

In reacting this way, Laura's mother was really teaching the child that she need not misbehave in order to assure herself of her mother's attention and love. It is very, very important to reward your children's good behavior and generous impulses with affection and encouragement. In this way, the child will eventually come to know that his parents do, indeed, love him despite the divorce. With this newfcund sense of security, the child's need to misbehave will eventually disappear.

Obviously, children of different ages will act out in different ways. Teen-agers can be especially annoying to their parents at times, with their amazing instinct for knowing how best to upset and worry their parents. Also, one cannot easily distract an adolescent, as one can a four-year-old.

But the same basic principles apply to adolescent acting out as to the misbehavior of younger children. Difficult as this may be in practice, parents should try to ignore the relatively minor rule infractions, temper tantrums, and general surliness of the adolescent in this situation. I realize that a torrent of verbal abuse from an adolescent son or daughter can be very hard for a parent to take. But to respond in kind is only to encourage further outbursts from your child. You really should attempt either to ignore the outburst or, if you feel it appropriate, to respond to it calmly and rationally. At the same time, you should be careful to reward the adolescent's positive behavior with affection and enthusiasm. Though they may seem somewhat mature and self-sufficient, adolescents desperately need to be assured of their parents' love.

There is some adolescent acting out that is self-destructive and simply cannot be ignored. We have already pointed out drug and alcohol abuse as the two most dramatic examples of this. Other behavior that truly harms the child — frequent school truancy, for example, or compulsively promiscuous sexual behavior — calls for the parents' calm but firm intervention. A parent, after all, is responsible for his child's welfare. If it is necessary to lay down reasonable rules governing the adolescent's social life, or if it is advisable to confer with the adolescent's teachers or counselors, these things should be done. Again, however, it is important that the adolescent see that his parents are acting, not out of rage or selfishness, but calmly and rationally. The parents should make it clear that they are acting out of love. Most adolescents will come to recognize the truth of this.

The defense mechanism called *regression* requires some explanation, since it frequently puzzles and embarrasses parents. Regression occurs when a child, instead of growing more mature, seems to move backward to an earlier stage of development. Regression can occur at any age and is not infrequently found in adults in crisis. The four-year-old may suddenly decide to drink his milk from his old baby's bottle. The fairly independent seven-year-old may suddenly become whiny and literally cling to his mother's skirts, afraid to be out of her sight. Older children may suddenly revert to baby talk, and imitate the behavior of their younger brothers and sisters.

Regression is really a subconscious attempt on the child's part to return to the good old days. Confused and threatened by the change that divorce has occasioned in his life, the child seeks to regain a time in the past when these conflicts and problems did not exist. The child envies the infant or very young child, whose every need, he thinks, is fully met by his parents, and who has no problems.

Regression should be treated by the parent as he or she would treat an undesirable acting-out behavior. The parent should, of course, allow the child a reasonable period of time to see if the problem will work itself out. Remember, you *and* your child are apt to be upset for some time during and after the divorce. The symptoms of this upset become a source of real concern only if they do not improve with time, and if they interfere with the child's ability to lead a normal life.

When regression seems to be a real and lasting problem, the parent should employ the principles discussed earlier. Immature behavior should be ignored, or calmly discouraged. Mature behavior should be rewarded with praise, attention, and affection.

We have seen, then, that a child may react to divorce in any one — or a combination — of several sometimes puzzling ways. It may not always be easy for you, the parent, to recognize your child's erratic or troubling behavior for what it is: an attempt to cope with his fear, anger, and sadness over the divorce situation. The important thing is for you not to overreact to these problems. If you can put your own anxiety or guilt aside and look for your child's behavioral clues as described in this chapter, both you and your child will have taken a giant step toward solving your problems together.

6

When You Resume
Your Social Life

AT SOME POINT after your separation or divorce, perhaps when the initial emotional shock and complications have been worked through, you will naturally start to think about exploring new relationships. For both the divorced parent and the children, this new beginning is one without precedent in their experience. In this chapter I will try to touch on some of the ways a new parent's re-entry into the social world of the single adult will affect the children — and how the children will affect the parent's social situation.

The first question that will confront the newly single parent about his or her *own* emotional future is: "When is it O.K. or appropriate for me to begin dating?" The answer seems overly simple: when you feel *ready* for it. For some parents, it will seem natural and desirable to seek out the company of the opposite sex once they have been formally separated from their spouse, or once formal divorce proceedings have been instituted with the courts. Other parents, perhaps for religious, social, or cultural reasons, do not feel that dating is appropriate until the divorce decree is final. This is purely a matter of conscience, strictly up to the individual.

From the child's psychological point of view, I think it's safe to say that a parent's dating may begin whenever, in the separated parent's mind, the separation is final. By that I mean final in an emotional, rather than a legal, sense. Once your marriage is irretrievably broken, there is no point in keeping the truth of your renewed social life from the child. As we have seen, failure to confront painful truths only confuses a child and leads to the development of reconciliation fantasies. Thus, from the viewpoint of the child's emotional welfare, there is no advantage to postponing your social life until the judge signs a final decree.

Clearly, the divorced parent's dating situation depends on how much time the parent is allowed to spend with the child. Take the case in which a father has sole custody of his children, and his ex-wife brings them to her home only to spend alternate weekends. This is perhaps the simplest case to manage, from the noncustodial parent's point of view.

First of all, if the mother in this instance has the company of her children only two days out of every fourteen, she may readily decide to forgo casual dating for those two days and devote herself exclusively to the children. This would certainly be true in the early weeks and months after the divorce. Of course, there's no ironclad rule that says a parent *must* forgo dating in such a situation. But parenting is, after all, the major priority of those visiting days. Except for special occasions, it might be better to forgo casual socializing on these weekends.

For couples who have won joint custody, parenting is obviously the priority of choice for both of them. They, too, will have to make value judgments about those occasions on which casual dating conflicts with child-care time. In doing so, of course, parents must take into account the child's age, temperament, and stage of adjustment to the divorce. Generally, in joint-custody cases, both parents can be assured of having adequate time with their children without feeling unduly guilty about leaving them with a baby sitter from time to time.

The most difficult situation, of course, is that faced by the man or woman — and it is still usually a woman — who finds herself with sole custody of her children. Such a woman can hardly be expected to forgo dating and social activities or to try to work a rare date to coincide with the children's biweekly visits to their father.

Once the custodial parent has worked through some of her own negative feelings about her divorce, she is still faced with two difficult questions: "How am I going to introduce my children to my new men friends? And how should I introduce these men to the children?" Sometimes these complications themselves seem so daunting that they prevent divorced mothers (and fathers) from seeking out a new social life.

No doubt some of this apprehension is well-founded. In addition, many divorced mothers complain that attractive men are frightened off when they learn that these women have children at home. Of course, there can be many reasons for this reaction. Many men, divorced or widowed, have children of their own to care for and can't even begin to face the emotional, or possibly the financial, problem of helping to raise stepchildren. Others may fear that a woman with children will be overeager to marry again, presumably to ease her own financial and emotional burden. Still others may simply not care for children or want to make parenting of any sort a part of their lives.

Of course, divorced fathers will often encounter much the same reactions from women, particularly where the father is the custodial parent. Women who have no children of their own may well be reluctant to take on the role of full-time stepmother to someone else's children. Women with children may fear that the stepsibling relationship is simply too complicated or emotionally perilous.

However, since divorced mothers still, in most cases, retain custody of their children, it is the mother who sometimes comes to feel that her children are a liability or disadvantage to her in the dating situation. And if, as sometimes happens, an attractive man backs off when he learns about the children, the newly divorced and quite possibly lonely mother is apt to be discouraged indeed.

In fact, some divorced parents become so concerned about eliciting a negative reaction from a date when they mention their children that they simply don't mention them at all! These parents seem to feel that, if they first establish a positive relationship with a new partner, they will eventually find a favorable moment to announce their children's existence.

A divorced parent should never deliberately withhold the fact that he or she has children in hope of finding the right moment to reveal their existence to a prospective partner. The fact that you are a parent is an important component of your identity. You should make it known fairly early in any meaningful relationship.

Whatever their ages, your children are going to be very curious about your new single status, and very curious about your social life. Moreover, since even very young children have sexual feelings and are aware, in some ways, of sexual behavior between men and women, a good deal of your children's curiosity may center around your sexual behavior.

By and large, in the matter of dating, the same general rule applies to children as applies to the man or woman you're seeing. That is, you should not lie to your children about your social life. You should always be willing to tell them that you're going out and with whom you're going. Any attempt to keep these very basic facts a mystery can cause enormous anxiety in children. Your child will be much more comfortable with the plain, unmysterious fact that you are going out to the movies with your friend Mr. X.

There is, however, no reason for your social acquaintances or even casual lovers to get to know your children or to spend any significant amount of time with them *unless* your relationship becomes an important part of your life. It is unnecessary and even unwise for you to introduce every casual date to your children and encourage every friend to act like one of the family. Such activity can confuse your child and, more important, can cause emotional damage by reopening recent wounds.

We must keep in mind that the child of divorce has already endured one very difficult separation. In the course of separation and divorce proceedings, one of his parents has physically left the home. This physical departure by a parent, the loss of that parent's constant and immediate presence, will almost certainly be the cause of some pain for the child. No matter how civil or reasonable divorcing parents are, there is no such thing as a totally painless divorce — not for the child of divorce or for his parents.

The parent's departure from the home will naturally cause the child to experience initial feelings of abandonment or loss. In time, with both parents' love and understanding, the child's emotional hurt will heal, and he will reconcile himself to his new living situation.

The custodial parent, however, may unwittingly reopen the child's wounds by attempting to inject every new social acquaintance and casual date into the family's life. For example, the child who lives with his father, and who naturally misses his noncustodial mother, is apt to be confused and hurt if he is encouraged to form emotional attachments to a succession of his father's woman friends. Such a child could develop feelings of affection for a woman who frequently visits his home and participates in some family activities. These loving feelings, in themselves, are healthy and positive. A serious problem arises, however, if the custodial parent ends his relationship with his woman friend, and she abruptly disappears from the child's life. The child is quite likely, in such a case, to re-experience all the painful feelings of abandonment and trauma he encountered when his mother left the home.

The situation becomes even more complicated and potentially harmful when the dating parent, over a period of time, introduces a number of opposite-sex friends or lovers into the family unit. Here the child may form attachments to several of these adult figures, only to be abandoned time and time again when his parent's relationships end with each of them.

A child who is forced to experience these painful emotions after already coping with the absence of one of his parents can suffer serious emotional harm. Some children who live through repeated episodes of this type of attachment/separation experience become terribly insecure. They live in constant fear of being deserted by every adult they have come to love and depend upon. Such children may experience anxiety symptoms, like nightmares, bed-wetting, and crying spells, and clinging behavior, like school avoidance.

Other children affected by these experiences may exhibit what is apparently the opposite reaction: an exaggerated sense of emotional independence and isolation, coupled with a basic suspicion of all new relationships. They may find it difficult to trust anyone and are likely to have a difficult time forming friendships with peers or classmates, as well as with significant adults in their lives.

Nine-year-old Eddie was one such emotionally isolated child. Eddie's mother had retained custody of her only child after a bitter divorce, and the boy saw his father only during school vacation periods. His mother, an attractive, outgoing woman, established an active and rewarding social life within the first year after her divorce.

She was acutely concerned about her son's lack of older male companionship and guidance, so to compensate for this, she encouraged each of her male friends to become involved with the boy, who seemed to enjoy the attention. Finally, however, after the child's mother ended two brief but intense relationships within the space of ten months, it became evident that Eddie's attitudes and behavior had changed. While he had previously been an easygoing, popular child, Eddie now became a loner. He was frequently angry or belligerent, and his teachers labeled him a disruptive influence in the classroom. Refusing to share his feelings with his mother, Eddie even refused to meet any new friends she invited to the house.

In this case, Eddie's anger and isolation stemmed from his anguish at having found — and then lost — the attention and friendship of two different adult males so shortly after his parents' divorce. The child's angry, independent attitude was a defense; by preventing himself from forming new friendships, the boy also protected himself from the pain of another loss.

As a rule, it is younger children who are most hurt by these real or imagined abandonments. Adolescents are generally sophisticated enough to show more understanding of their parents' social situation. But teen-agers, too, may have some difficulty if they are expected to feel that each one of their parents' opposite-sex friends must be treated as a member of the family.

What, then, *is* a natural, unforced relationship between a divorced parent's children and the parent's new social or romantic interest?

At the outset of the dating process, there's really no need for your child and your friend to have much of a relationship at all. If it is natural for your date to call for you at home, by all means he or she should be introduced to the children. At this point, however, such contacts should be kept fairly brief and matter-of-fact. On the other hand, you should not keep your dating a secret. Children are quick to uncover a secret; they are also likely to be troubled by the feeling that the parent is deliberately keeping something a mystery. If they do not actually meet your date, a simple explanation such as "I am going out to dinner tonight with so-and-so" will be sufficient at first. Of course, the emotional tenor of his situation will naturally change if your relationship intensifies.

A new variation on this problem is presented when the parent decides to renew his sex life with a new partner. All children have a natural curiosity about the love or sexual activities that take place between men and women. Though many children are reluctant to ask questions about the love relationship between their biological parents, the parent's dating habits after the divorce raise these issues again, in a particularly compelling way.

It is not necessary for a parent to describe in detail every romantic or sexual interlude that occurs in his or her post-divorce social life. But the parent must understand that the child's questions about the parent's way of expressing affection or sexual feelings indicate a perfectly normal curiosity.

On the whole, it is probably best to be as honest with your child on this subject as you comfortably can be. Obvious avoidance of the child's questions, or displays of extreme discomfort or anger, will certainly not cure the child's curiosity. They will probably have just the opposite result.

Children, after all, have a very rich fantasy life and can imagine highly colorful — even lurid — answers and explanations for things they find puzzling when true information is withheld from them. Those of us who can still remember certain schoolyard rumors about sex that made the rounds when we were children can attest to the vivid imagery that children can all too easily substitute for missing facts.

Presumably, children old enough to be curious have already had explained to them the basic physical and emotional components of human sexuality and reproduction. Since they have, I hope, received that information from you rather than from sensational schoolyard gossip, they already have a background that predisposes them to see that sexual behavior takes place in a loving, sharing context.

It would seem, then, that the parent must strike her own balance between total honesty and her right to privacy. Simple questions such as "Do you and Mr. So-and-So kiss when you go out?" might easily be answered honestly and matter-of-factly. On the other hand, casual or short-lived sexual encounters with a person who will never occupy an important place in the lives of you or your children need not be a subject of discussion. Depending on the child's age and the sexual attitudes he has grown up with, disclosure of such sexual encounters may, in fact, only confuse or disturb him. Obviously, however, this is an area in which each parent must make his or her own decisions. Your criteria for dealing with your children in this area will depend largely on what you consider to be the desirable moral and emotional climate of your home.

The one central problem to look for, in this matter of the parent's sexual behavior, is that point at which the child appears to be more troubled by his suspicions and fantasies, caused by *lack* of information, than he would be by a calm, low-keyed explanation of the truth.

One very obvious example of this, and the example most frequently cited by psychiatrists, is the situation in which the very young child hears two adults — usually his parents — during their lovemaking. This can happen easily enough, when the child hears the sounds of lovemaking coming from his parents' bedroom, or when he is actually in that bedroom and thought to be sleeping. Most often, the small child who overhears the sounds of a couple's passion during lovemaking will not be able to understand the emotions the two adults are experiencing. Instead, the child will mistake the sounds of passion and love for the sounds of violence. He will assume that his parents are having a physical battle and are hurting each other. If he should happen actually to witness the scene, he will probably assume that his father is physically harming his mother.

Needless to say, these perceptions will greatly alarm and distress the child, and this possibility is one among many reasons why, as parents, you should be careful to communicate to your children the truth about sexual love, answering their basic questions about sex all along. These questions are likely to arise without regard to your living situation, for even if you, as a single parent, have been completely celibate during your separation, your child's natural curiosity about sex will have been piqued by everything from sexual scenes on television to the normal talk and questions of his peers.

What you tell your child about sex will depend largely on the child's age and ability to comprehend the physical facts. For a three- or four-year-old it is often enough to know that "babies come from their mommy's tummy." On the other hand, a child approaching puberty can understand — and needs — much more information to help him cope with the changes his own body is undergoing.

When you, as a single parent, become romantically or sexually involved with another person and when that relationship takes place partly in your home, it will be best to tell your children the truth about physical love between the two of you. Unavoidably, your child by this time will be giving a great deal of thought to the sexual relationship between you and your partner. And if sexual activity is going on, chances are that you are sleeping together or making love in your bedroom. If that is the case, it then becomes highly strained and almost ridiculously artificial to pretend that "nothing's happening" in Mommy's or Daddy's bedroom.

But the point here is that while honesty sometimes dictates the statement that "Mommy and [her friend] do love each other in bed," it is not necessary — and indeed may be harmful — for the parent to describe the details of her own specific sexual activity. Parents, it must be remembered, do have a right to privacy in these most intimate aspects of their lives. Not only does the child have to learn to respect the privacy of adults, but this is simply more information, and more of the wrong kind of information, than a child can deal with emotionally. Such disclosures transcend the bound of simple honesty and openness. They almost make the child an emotional participant in his parent's lovemaking. This will almost certainly trigger guilt and anxiety in a child, no matter what his age. Our previous discussion of the oedipal phase and of incest taboos is very relevant here.

Of course, intensified emotional intimacy between a parent and lover confronts the family with many more ramifications. These deeper relationships will be discussed in the next chapter.

The one question that most troubles parents about their post-divorce social life is: "How will it affect my child emotionally?" I will repeat here the message of earlier chapters: A child's reaction to his parent's behavior will vary greatly according to the age and individual temperament of the child. But even keeping in mind all the developmental stages discussed earlier in this book, it is crucial to note that a child's feelings and reactions to one parent's dating will be influenced enormously by the attitude of his other parent.

Unfortunately, post-divorce dating provides another favorite battleground for divorced couples. And once again, the victim of that battle will be the child.

It is not uncommon to see cases in which the ex-spouse has behaved amicably throughout the period of separation and divorce, only to display animosity and jealousy when one party or the other starts dating. This happens, usually, because of unresolved feelings of anger and resentment against the dating spouse. This anger may date back to well before the divorce, and may just never have been expressed through the amicable veneer. Or the nondating spouse may feel tied down by the children or by her financial situation, and envy her ex-husband's apparent freedom.

These angry feelings are natural and understandable reactions to a complex emotional situation. For one thing, a man or woman who has spent important years of his or her life with a partner, and parented children by that partner, almost always maintains, understandably, a vaguely possessive interest in the activities and welfare of the partner. In a truly amicable divorce, where many of the negative emotions have been worked through, that interest may take the form of continued friendly contact and the exchange of current information. But this slightly possessive feeling sometimes exists even in the most acrimonious of divorces, where the former spouses maintain that they actually hate each other; indeed, such cases are prime examples of what are called love/hate relationships. And sometimes, the former spouse does not even consciously realize that he feels that possessive twinge for his ex-partner until someone new displays the same, overtly possessive interest — until, in other words, the ex-partner begins to date.

Furthermore, dating may point up the differences and relative advantages of the respective ex-spouses' lifestyles. While one parent may have wanted, and been quite happy to receive, sole custody of the children, his ex-partner's frequent socializing may make his parenting responsibilities seem more restrictive. Or a divorced father, paying alimony and/or child support, may not feel that he can financially afford to date. He may feel envious of his ex-wife's seeming freedom from worry in this area, if he thinks she is being wined and dined by other men.

Finally, there will be a great deal of natural curiosity on the parent's part to find out exactly what sort of person his ex-spouse is replacing him with. There may be a tendency to make comparisons, favorable or unfavorable.

From all of these feelings will flow the temptation to use the visiting child as a spy or informant, to question the child about his knowledge of "Who are Mommy's friends?" and "What do they do?" There may also be a temptation to use the dating situation to express criticism of the other parent either directly or indirectly.

In this regard, I would ask you to reread chapter 3, "Games Parents Play," and adhere to the principles discussed there. Do not allow the dating situation to become an area of conflict between you and your ex-mate. If you do, it is your child who stands to lose the most. Encourage your child to treat your ex-mate's friends politely and with respect; do not set up a conflict of loyalty for the child.

You, yourself, might also want to keep an open mind about your ex-spouse's choice of romantic friends. For, as we shall see, you might one day find yourself dealing with such a friend as a member of your child's new stepfamily.

7

Your New Partner and
Your Children

THE TRANSITION from date to stepparent involves dramatic changes in the emotional life of all family members. But some of these changes can be introduced gradually and naturally. When you first sense that a man or woman is becoming a central part of your life, it is appropriate and even necessary to share some aspects of your family life with that person. It is only right and fair that your children understand some of your feelings about your lover, and that he or she come to experience something of your family life. In a healthy supportive partnership, it is impossible and undesirable to completely divide one's life and attention into separate categories of "family" and "lover." Such a division, even if possible, would be artificial and strained, and would hamper your — and your partner's — emotional growth.

As your involvement deepens, it is best to allow your lover and your children to come to know each other in a gradual, natural way. This, it must be admitted, is more easily said than done. Given the circumstances, it is almost certain that all parties concerned — parent, parent's lover, children — will at first be quite tense.

In these initial meetings, it is understandable that everyone should be at least a bit nervous or apprehensive. Let's look at the scene from each individual's point of view:

1. The involved *parent* desperately wants the two halves of his life to come together, i.e., for his children to like and accept his new partner, and vice versa.
2. The concerned *partner*, acutely aware of the importance of being liked and accepted by the children, will bear the uncomfortable knowledge of being minutely looked over and judged by these children.
3. The *children* by now have sensed that this new partner is a very important figure in their parent's life. They will be extremely curious, and uncertain about the exact role the partner will play in their own lives.

In short, no parent planning to introduce a lover or potential spouse to his or her children should expect the first meetings to produce instant rapport. Be patient with yourself, your mate, and your children.

Your partner's first social sessions with your children should be planned to be as relaxed as possible. It's probably not a good idea to start out with an evening at home, where adults and children will end up sitting in the living room and staring at one another, searching for a way to make conversation. Children are often shy around any unfamiliar adult, and casual conversation is not a child's strongest point. Prospective stepparents should not be disappointed, therefore, when their partner's children seem tongue-tied or answer in detached, one-syllable words.

Frederick, an airline pilot and thirty-five-year-old bachelor who had been dating Helen, a divorced mother of two young boys, for nearly a year, had no prior personal experience with children. Frederick was very intimidated by the thought of having to obtain the children's approval.

"That first whole evening together, we had dinner and then sat in the TV room. Helen had made the boys' favorite dinner and dessert, and I'd brought along an armful of presents — model airplanes and other things Helen had told me they liked.

"Dinner was pretty uncomfortable — the boys mostly just stared at me. But afterward, I really tried to make conversation. I told them how I'd been trained as a pilot in the navy, about some close calls I'd had landing on carriers — all the stuff I hoped would interest them.

"But the older boy, Charlie, just stared at me, nodding politely. I could tell he was bored. And Kevin, the little one, didn't even keep up a pretense — he was glued to the TV for the entire evening. I felt that I'd bombed out. I was miserable."

Later, in talking it over, Helen and Frederick decided that perhaps they had expected too much from the boys too soon. They agreed to plan for more meetings where the boys could simply "look Fred over" without being expected to perform socially.

"We started out taking the kids to movies," Frederick later recounted. "They enjoyed that, and it gave them a chance to get used to me without being forced into extended conversations. Later, if I came over for the evening, I'd usually bring a model plane that the three of us could assemble that night. I also took the boys up in my own four-seater plane a few times — they got a real kick out of that. That way, we gradually got to feel more comfortable together."

After one false start, Helen and Frederick hit upon the best way to introduce a potential stepparent into the family. Rather than create an artificial atmosphere where everyone felt constrained to be on their best behavior, they started out with low-pressure situations, such as going to the movies, where relatively little interaction was required of the children. Then, after the boys had become somewhat more comfortable in his presence, Frederick structured his visits around an area of mutual interest — airplanes and flying.

Generally speaking, these outlines might well be followed by any family trying to get to know and accept a future stepparent. The first meetings will probably be less painful and more productive if they are centered around an organized activity, such as a movie or show, a day trip or visit to the zoo. Any activity that can serve as the focus of attention will do. These first meetings will serve the purpose of allowing the children to size up the new adult, and vice versa, without building up too much social pressure to be polite and to be friendly.

This occasion gives all parties the necessary time to become more comfortable in one another's presence. Then, when the initial awkwardness is gone, the children and adults will feel confident enough to talk to and enter into games with one another. During these times they will lay the foundation for their relationships for years to come.

Frederick, you will remember, when he arrived to spend his first evening with Helen's children, was carrying "an armful of presents." The question that often arises is when is it useful for a potential stepparent, or even a casual friend, to bring along gifts for his date's children.

Ordinary sensitivity to the family situation, and his place in it, should allow Frederick and others in his situation to gauge the point at which gift-giving is a healthy and positive thing. As a rule, it certainly doesn't harm a child to receive a small gift. Children love little surprises, and an inexpensive game or toy might serve to remind the child that he, too — not only his parent — is important to the prospective stepparent.

However, it can actually be counterproductive to overdo the gift giving. The man or woman who constantly appears at the door with too many — or very expensive — gifts may be creating a situation that will backfire at some point. In this situation, both the child and the gift giver come to see the gifts as bribes. The adult may be trying to buy the child's love; he may feel unworthy of his new family, or guilty about replacing the biological parent. Compulsive gift giving then becomes, in his view, the only way he can make himself worthy in the child's eyes.

This problem of compulsive gift giving also works to the child's emotional disadvantage. After all, the child is well aware that it is very important to her parent, and to his or her new partner, that she accept the partner into the family. Children are very sensitive, and most will understand their own power in these circumstances; the child's adamant disapproval of the new partner can complicate the stepfamily's life enormously.

Sensing this, the child may, consciously or subconsciously, put herself in the position of blackmailing the prospective stepparent. She may actually, in actions rather than in words, encourage the new adult in her life to buy her love with even bigger and more expensive gifts.

Such a situation will, in the end, make both child and adult very unhappy. The future stepparent will feel exploited and resentful; the child will feel guilty and unhappy. These negative feelings will hamper the establishment of a truly affectionate and honest stepparent-child relationship.

In discussing the most natural way to introduce a prospective stepparent into the family, we tend to assume that, with time and patience, the child will eventually come to some acceptance of her parent's prospective spouse. Unfortunately, this is not always the case.

Perhaps the most painful and conflict-ridden situation divorced parents can face occurs when their children refuse to accept the person they love and want to marry. Sometimes, despite the best and most generous efforts of the prospective spouse, children remain unyielding in their disapproval of their parent's intended spouse. At best, this creates an uncomfortable situation; at worst, a tragic one.

Sadly, many divorced parents abandon plans to marry people they love very much because of the intransigence of their children. These people assume that marriage under such circumstances would be an emotional disaster for the entire family.

We all know of friends and acquaintances who have sacrificed their own happiness in these situations to accommodate what they honestly believe to be their children's best interests. Many of these parents carry this regret throughout life, measuring their years of loneliness and sacrifice against what might have been. What many parents never know is that their children, particularly with the hindsight that early adulthood brings, carry similarly painful burdens of guilt and recrimination. A young woman named Marie recalled, when she was twenty, her feelings about her divorced mother's suitor:

"I guess we just refused — my brother and I — to admit that my parents really were divorced — finally, permanently, divorced. We missed Dad a lot, though we visited him twice a month. What's more, we resented every male friend Mother ever brought into our home.

"Two years after the divorce, Mom started seeing Mark, a middle-aged widower who ran a small business in town. For some reason, when my brother and I finally realized that Mom was serious about Mark, we sort of panicked. We were determined to keep him out of our home and out of our lives.

"After that neither Mark nor Mom could do anything right, as far as we were concerned. We found fault with Mark's appearance, his opinions, his manners, even the gifts he brought us. After a while, we told Mom outright that we would never accept Mark as a member of our household, let alone as a father.

"Mom never told us what happened, but soon she just stopped seeing him. That was a dozen or so years ago. Since then, Mom's dated casually, but she never married again and says she never will. Mark did remarry several years ago — Mom didn't say a thing about it, I just happened to see it in the local paper.

"She's getting older now and I know she's lonely. I've felt terrible about her for years now. If we hadn't been so selfish and obnoxious, I'm sure she'd have a happier life today."

These feelings are not uncommon when a child is allowed to exercise a veto over his parent's intended spouse. It is certainly understandable that a caring parent, who probably already carries some feelings of guilt over having put the children through a divorce, is reluctant to subject those children to a new stepfather they claim vociferously to hate. Generally, I believe this sort of parental sacrifice is a mistake.

We have discussed, at length, the childhood stage of magical thinking and the many situations in which the child's illusions about his "all-powerful" wishes and thoughts can cause him enormous grief and anxiety. A young child may, for example, have angry thoughts about his mother, and feel that these "bad thoughts" were responsible if the mother leaves her family during divorce or marital separation.

We've also seen how, during the child's oedipal phase, he or she will develop very strong possessive feelings for the opposite-sex parent. In the normal order of events, these feelings will be resolved and the child will learn, in the course of his emotional and sexual development, to transfer these special feelings to other members of the opposite sex. But should the child feel that he has actually won the oedipal struggle — won Mommy away from Daddy, for example, by causing them to divorce — the resulting guilt feelings will be very hard for the child to deal with.

All of these considerations come into play again, when the

divorced parent makes known his or her intention to remarry. For a variety of reasons, the parent's children may not show immediate enthusiasm for the parent's plans, or his intended spouse. Ordinarily, the child's negative reaction has less to do with the character of the parent's new partner than it does with the child's own reunion fantasies, those powerful, sometimes hidden, wishes that the divorced parents will somehow reunite. These feelings tend to linger long after the child ceases to speak about them or act on them. As long as both parents remain unmarried, most children will entertain some hope, however slim, of parental reunion.

The one thing that *will* put an end to reunion fantasies is the remarriage of one or both parents. And, no matter how fond the child may be of his parent's intended spouse, he is quite likely to resent the fact that this new marriage will finally close the door on the comforting hope for a parental reconciliation.

By bringing together some of these fundamental truths about a child's way of thinking — the power of magical thinking, oedipal feelings, reunion fantasies — we can see some of the reasons why a child might initially want to veto his parent's remarriage. And we can also begin to see why the child's veto alone should not be allowed to determine whether or not his parent remarries.

We must assume, first, that the prospective spouse is a reasonably warm and attractive person with a genuine interest in stepparenting. (Clearly, there are people who are unfit for parenting of any sort, by reason of chronic mental illness, alcoholism, drug addiction, or a record of child abuse or spouse-battering. In these threatening situations, a child's objections manifest insight and common sense, and are to be listened to.) The much more common situation, however, is one in which children persistently and loudly protest their parent's partnership or marriage for reasons that seem inconsequential. Children may criticize the potential stepparent's physical appearance, or his speech mannerisms, or even his gifts and other attempts at pleasing them. They may constantly compare the new stepparent to their biological same-sex parent. These comparisons can be endless, trivial, and inevitably unfavorable. They sometimes shift — today the child will criticize the future stepparent's haircut; tomorrow he'll accept the haircut but criticize his taste in films. If these criticisms are constant and energetic, they can be extremely discouraging for both the divorced parent and his or her new partner.

Under these circumstances, it takes a certain amount of courage for the couple to marry. But they should marry, nonetheless, if they love each other and want to spend their lives together. In nearly all cases, the children will come around, though it may take as long as a year for this to happen. In any event, a parent who rejects a suitable and loving mate because his or her children object to the marriage is probably doing those children more harm than good — as we saw earlier in this chapter.

On the other hand, it would be unwise to consider marriage to a man or woman who disliked or had no interest in children. Such a person, no matter what his or her intentions, may well come to resent the stepchildren and consider them a burden.

Divorced parents frequently question their own motives in remarrying. If they feel the burden of single-parenting to be great, they may worry that they are marrying again just to have someone around who will share the burden. But there are many considerations that go into choosing a marital partner, and for the divorced parent, a partner's suitability and helpfulness as a stepparent is naturally going to be one of these considerations. The fact that remarriage can relieve a parent of some of the burdens of single-parenting is no cause for guilt. Finding someone to love who also promises to become a positive part of your children's lives is a happy event, indeed.

Assume now that all preliminary steps have been taken: The

potential stepparent has gotten to know the children (and vice versa), living arrangements have been settled upon, the wedding ceremony has been performed, the new stepfamily has officially become a unit. If possible, the new husband and wife would do well to allow themselves a grace period — the traditional honeymoon away from relatives and friends.

Many remarried couples with children skip the honeymoon period entirely, for practical reasons of family or finances. Other couples make their honeymoon literally a family affair, and take their children along for a short trip. Certainly, either of these choices may be perfectly fine and sensible; there are no rules that need to be followed here.

If circumstances permit, however, the newly married couple with stepchildren would be well advised to take a short honeymoon away from home, and by themselves. If the children of the family can spend this period with relatives or close friends, a brief separation will not do emotional harm. And a traditional honeymoon will put the children of this marriage on notice that the parent and new stepparent are special *to each other* as husband and wife and deserve some time alone together.

Living in a family as a stepparent has a very different emotional flavor from being a frequent visitor to the children's home, or even from being their special friend. A stepparent is a figure of substantial authority, with substantial responsibilities. Is there any special preparation the new stepparent can take, to make the transition easier or smoother?

The first and crucial step may seem painfully obvious: The stepparent should educate himself or herself concerning the emotional and physical stages of child development, paying particular attention to the developmental periods that the stepchildren are currently experiencing.

Many people think of parenting as a skill that comes automatically from being in the presence of children. And it is true that a parent's relationship with an individual child will depend partly on instinct and personality, as relationships between adults do. But there are many, many things about the working of a child's mind and the emotional effects of his physical development that a stepparent unfamiliar with children simply cannot immediately absorb, no matter how conscientious and well-intended he or she is.

For example, how can a person unfamiliar with child development hope to cope calmly and knowledgeably with the "terrible twos," that perfectly normal burst of physical and intellectual growth that makes two-year-old children try the patience and physical stamina of every parent? How is the brand-new step-parent to understand the secretive and sometimes worrisome behavior of some children at puberty? Or cope calmly with the energy and recklessness and rebellion of adolescence?

Fortunately, there are any number of good books on all stages of child development. I suggest that a childless stepparent *and* the biological parent read one or more of these books *before* the wedding. Reading such material together and discussing it with each other can be very helpful to the new couple. This experience gives the new husband and wife a context in which to share observations, questions, and even doubts or misgivings about the children.

One valuable and very common insight that may come out of such discussions was articulated recently by James, a childless, twice-divorced man who was planning to marry Sheila, the mother of two teen-aged boys. "I've loved Sheila almost from the first moment I met her," James stated. "And, after a while, I got to like the boys. I'd take them to the ballpark when the home team was in town, or we'd go to the movies — that sort of thing.

"But after Sheila and I set the wedding date, I found myself getting impatient with the kids. It suddenly seemed to me that

Sheila pampered them too much, or that they were too demanding, or something. Once I sort of hinted that they should spend more weekends with their father, even though I knew he lived out-of-state. That was the first real argument Sheila and I ever had.

"About a month before the wedding I was so resentful of the boys that I really feared for our planned marriage. So I went for a few sessions with a counselor who was recommended by a friend.

"Almost immediately, in talking with him, I realized the problem — it was so obvious that I was almost embarrassed by it.

"It was just that, well, both boys strongly resembled their father — same coloring, facial structure, same build. So every time I looked at the kids, all I could think of was their father and Sheila, in bed together. It sounds stupid, but living with the kids was a constant reminder that the woman I loved had once loved someone else."

James's jealousy and resentment of his wife's children is not uncommon. While few people admit it, new spouses do sometimes see in their stepchildren a nagging reminder of their spouse's previous marriage and sexual activity. This feeling may be an emotional overreaction, but it is not, to use James's word, *stupid*. Fortunately, once it is recognized this feeling can be dealt with fairly easily. Irrational resentment of one's stepchildren generally dissipates once the stepparent acknowledges its cause.

While it is important for the stepparent to educate himself or herself regarding the developmental processes in children, most of the day-to-day parenting skills that will build the bond of affection, authority, and trust between stepparent and child are of the practical sort, often learned by trial and error. Time, patience, and effort are the qualities most important here. Love and trust cannot be forced on anyone — child or adult. Children, especially those who have experienced parental divorce, may seem reluctant at first to accept or offer affection to a new adult in their lives. These children *want* love, and will accept proffered love, but only after they've had the time to convince themselves that the love offered is genuine and can be trusted.

These considerations tell us a good deal about how the new stepparent should approach the child and the sort of initial reactions he or she might expect.

One thing now-grown stepchildren recall is the great significance of some forms of address — "Mother," "Father," and so on — and their gratitude and relief at not being forced, at the outset, to address the stepparents as "Mom" or "Dad." The question of how to address a new stepparent is one that the adults sometimes misinterpret. The biological parent or stepparent may feel that the child's reluctance to call a new stepparent by a parental title is a mark of dislike or disrespect. Sometimes, after an attempt at persuasion has failed, parents try to lay down the law: "You *will* call your stepfather 'Dad' or else!"

This approach almost always proves disastrous. Many children, whenever confronted with an "or-else" ultimatum, will opt for the "or else." More important, forcing a child to address a new stepparent as if he were the biological parent can only make the child feel resentment and dislike. Unless the child has lost all contact with his biological parent in infancy or very early childhood, he will remember his biological mother and father as very special and irreplaceable figures in his life. This is sometimes true even of children who have been orphaned early in life and have only vague recall of their biological parents. Certainly an older child who loses a parent through death continues to feel a strong emotional tie to that parent.

The child of divorce, then, will always have some special ties of love and loyalty to his living biological parents — even where one of the parents has behaved badly or irresponsibly, or even where he has abused or abandoned the family. The child's love may be generously laced with grief and fury, but the image of the biological parent will nonetheless be rooted somewhere in the child's emotional history.

For an adult to insist from the beginning of the stepfamily relationship that he be addressed as "Father," or she as "Mother," may create confusion and a conflict of loyalties in the child, who is very likely to feel that he is being asked to abandon his real biological parent and to transfer that special child-parent allegiance to the new adult in his life.

Understandably, the child may become resentful and angry with the stepparent if this struggle over titles persists. A child simply cannot be *forced* to view the stepparent with precisely the same respect and affection that he may accord a *biological* parent. The reason is very simple: A stepparent, at least to a child past the toddler stage, *is not and will never be exactly the same as a biological parent.* Nor should the stepmother or stepfather try to be.

The emotional roles that the stepparent *can* fill are as rich and more varied than the biological parent role. We've seen examples of stepchildren who came to love and see stepparents as either aunt/uncle, coach/confidante, big sister/brother, friend/social arbiter.

These are valuable roles the stepparent *can* play without trying to compete emotionally with the biological parent. They are highly individual roles, varying greatly from child to child and family to family. Forcing the child immediately to accept the stepparent as "mother" or "father" adults actually interferes with the development of a healthy, affectionate stepparent/stepchild relationship. That relationship may assume one of many forms and must be allowed freedom to find its own emotional tenor over time.

How shall the new stepfamily decide about parental titles? The most fruitful and promising way is to leave all possible options open. If the stepchild first is allowed to employ a neutral, value-free form of address, he will not feel bullied or coerced into pretending there's a new parent in the house, ready to replace his biological parent.

The most simple and obvious solution is to encourage your children to address the stepparent by his or her first name. Later on, usually after a few years together as a family unit, some children may indeed feel such warmth and affection toward their stepparents that they will begin to address them as "Mom" or "Dad." That is a very moving and genuine proof of a stepchild's love, but it is not the only proof.

Some parents, on principle, believe that children should not be allowed to address adults by their first names; some believe that this form of address indicates presumption or a lack of respect on the child's part. But the stepparent/child relationship is anything but formal. It is, or it will become, an intimate and overwhelmingly important part of the child's life. And while adults may, if they wish, try out compromise titles such as "Uncle" or "Aunt," these begin to ring false very shortly. It is best to avoid the artificiality of these attempts at family feeling. Allowing the child either to use the stepparent's first name or to find his own, hybrid affectionate nickname, will help to encourage mutual intimacy and respect.

Since children take comfort and security from the existence of a predictable, reliable environment, the changes that necessarily occur in the life of any new stepfamily are bound to be uncomfortable for them. This is most especially true for young children, but change also produces tension in older children and in most adults as well.

What most adults unfamiliar with children do not anticipate is that even the *tiniest* changes in a child's habits or lifestyle can seem to be, in the child's mind, an enormous disruption.

Any doting but childless friend or relative who has ever baby-sat with small children can attest to this. And even the parent who is very much accustomed to the particular habits and preferences of his own small children may find himself astonished to see an entirely new array of these demands made by his stepchildren.

"I remember the very first evening I spent alone with the kids," recalls Carla, who had recently married the custodial father of three- and five-year-old daughters. "Steve usually gave them their baths while I took care of the dishes. We'd only been married a few weeks, but I thought I knew about the bedtime ritual — give the kids a bath, read them a story, tuck them into bed. Simple, right? Wrong!

"Both the girls — Laura and Katie — understood that Steve had to stay late at the office and wouldn't be home till late. No problem there. And at eight o'clock on the dot — their regular time — I announced I would give them their baths. No problem there.

"By nine-thirty, an hour and a half later, I was completely traumatized. I felt like an ogre, an insensitive lout. I'd done everything wrong.

"First of all, it was a Tuesday night. I didn't know that Steve always washed the girls' hair on Saturday, Tuesday, and Thursday nights. When the girls told me — after I'd gotten them out of the tub — I suggested we skip it 'till tomorrow night.' This brought outraged protests. So, back into the tub they went.

"Of course, I used the wrong shampoo — they wanted the *herbal* shampoo, not the *regular* shampoo. The rinse water was too cold, they said. How was I to know? I didn't want to accidentally scald two little girls.

"Then — horror of horrors — I used the wrong bath towels to dry them. They always use the new Star Wars towels, not the old Raggedy Ann towels. Except on Mondays and Thursdays, of course, when the Star Wars towels are in the wash!

"It wasn't that the girls were nasty about it, or rude. They were really upset; they didn't understand how *anyone* could make such obvious mistakes. I began to feel that their faith in me was being sorely tested, indeed. I felt like a stranger to them. I *was* a stranger to them. By the time I tucked them into bed — the wrong way, of course — I felt like a total failure."

While it's highly doubtful that a child will suffer psychological harm from having her hair shampooed on Wednesday instead of Tuesday, or by being wrapped in one towel rather than another, it's also true that children take some measure of comfort from the sameness of daily routine. And it is simply impossible for a stepparent to enter into the child's family and immediately learn every tiny detail of the child's likes and dislikes.

And *tiny* details they are. Some kids prefer their hamburgers thick and round; others raise a fuss unless they're served large *flat* hamburgers. Some kids demand that their shoes be tied in a double knot; others will tolerate only single knots. Children have staunch opinions about how almost everything they eat, wear, or have done should be presented.

These little habits and preferences are not just a sign of will-fulness. A child wants something to be done a certain way because it has *always,* in his memory, been done that way — by the caretakers who came before the stepparent. And most often, one of the most important of those caretakers was the biological parent that you are now "replacing" in his household.

This is one reason why the new stepparent's unwitting deviations from the child's familiar habits can become a source of tension and conflict. Given time, normal healthy children certainly will adjust to the stepparent's own way of doing things, if the stepparent remains sensitive to the child's needs and personality.

But it must be remembered that the child, especially the young child, who has memories of being fed, bathed, and cared for by the biological parent has grown up believing that the biological parent's habits and manners were the only "right" habits and manners. A young child is simply not sophisticated enough to grasp the concept of separate but equal lifestyles. He cannot compare two different methods or styles and understand that, while they are not alike, they may be equally sensible or acceptable.

The stepparent's position is complicated by the fact that the children continue to spend some significant blocs of time with their noncustodial biological parent. Of course, the noncustodial parent, when he or she has the children, will care for their needs in the old familiar way. Thus Carla came to discover — as many stepparents do — that when the girls returned from a visit with their noncustodial mother, they were more critical than usual of Carla's way of doing things.

This behavior may be due to a conflict of loyalties. The little girls here were happy to spend a weekend, or part of a summer, with their biological mother. And when they were with her they did things the old way — the mother's way. No matter how much they were coming to love and adjust to Carla, these very young girls were always a bit confused when they returned to her. The unspoken question on their minds concerned their love for two different adult females who cared for them: If they allowed themselves to accept and appreciate their stepmother's ways, were they in some way emotionally abandoning their biological mother?

Of course, this conflict will be prolonged and aggravated if the noncustodial parent is openly hostile toward the stepparent. A parent who is still bitter and angry about the divorce may try to turn the children against the other biological parent. But if the parent senses that the children will not accept those negative feelings about the ex-spouse, he may find it emotionally "safer" and just as effective to try to poison the children's minds against the stepparent instead.

This is a vicious game that can really hurt children. Not only does it interfere with the child's acceptance of the stepparent; it causes him to question the love and devotion of all the important adults in his life.

There is very little the unjustly maligned stepparent can do in this situation but hope that time and persistent love and patience will allow the child to see the true situation for himself. The stepparent, however, should not display bitterness or other negative feelings about the biological parent who behaves in this hurtful and inappropriate fashion, for reasons that will be discussed in the next chapter.

And so, the new family begins after the courtship, after the awkward introductions, after the wedding, the honeymoon, the setting up of a new household. The next few years will be of supreme importance to this new family unit. Let's now examine the process of learning to be a family.

8

Stepfamilies: Emotional Growth in the First Years

OF THE MILLIONS of men and women who are divorced annually in this country, at least 60 to 75 percent will eventually enter into a new marriage. And of these remarriages, at least half will involve children born into the prior marriages of one or both new spouses.

The consequences of these statistics are truly mind boggling. For one thing, this extremely high incidence of divorce and remarriage over the last two decades has completely changed the romantic expectations and dreams of an entire generation. The old idea, expounded in countless novels and films of the 1950s, was as conventional and predictable as if it — as if life itself — had been set in concrete. Typically in the fiction of those and earlier days, a young man and woman completed their educations, courted (chastely), married, acquired a house and mortgage, and eventually, had children. In most romantic fiction of that period, the story ended there.

In the 1980s, that's where the real story, for many of us, only begins. The new tale is certainly more complicated and less neatly ordered than perhaps we'd like. But it definitely can be as rewarding, and perhaps even richer in texture and complexity, than the lives many of our parents and grandparents lived. A remarriage, particularly one involving children, requires something of a reordering of everyone's emotional universe. But if we are careful to educate ourselves about the meaning of our feelings and the feelings of others, our new stepfamilies will prove meaningful and precious to us.

Stepfamily. Stepmother. Stepchild. What awkward words, filled with less-than-pleasant associations. From the fairy tales of childhood we long ago learned that stepmothers were, at best, cold and remote, at worst, actually cruel and malicious. Stepchildren, naturally, were pitiful little beings who were either sadly neglected or actively abused. In any case, the stepfamily always seemed a somewhat unnatural or, at least, disadvantaged entity. Ideally, we might want to find a new, more positive term for these new families, just as we should find a substitute for the term *broken home.*

In any case, the word *stepfamily* can accurately describe a number of very different family constellations. The classic, and probably still the most common, example is the family in which the remarried wife brings her biological children into the home she shares with her new husband. Again classically, the new husband, while he may have biological children, probably does not have custody of those children.

But nowadays, particularly with the recent and substantial changes in the laws regarding child custody, a stepfamily may vary considerably from the model just described. The new wife may never have had children of her own, or she may have custody of those children. She may share joint custody with her ex-husband, or she may have split custody — custody of some but not all of the children. And, of course, all of these variations may also be true for her new husband. Consequently, there may be stepsiblings who live together or apart, or apart from at least some of their biological siblings. Round off this complicated range of possibilities with all of the respective possible step-grandparents, stepaunts and -uncles, cousins, and so on, and you can understand why some new stepparents find themselves overwhelmed and a bit frightened.

Consider just one example, that of Theresa, a thirty-four-old woman with a twelve-year-old son and eight-year-old daughter. On her divorce, Theresa and her ex-husband settled on a split-custody arrangement, with Theresa taking eight-year-old Debbie into her new home, and her ex-husband, Dan, continuing to live in their old house with twelve-year-old Tony. Within a few years, both Theresa and Dan had remarried and one of these new spouses had children of his own.

Theresa's new husband, George, had custody of his fifteen-year-old twin boys. Dan's wife, Roberta, had no children of her own.

Each of the persons mentioned above now found himself to be related in some way to *every one* of the others. Let's take them one at a time.

Theresa, in addition to her custodial daughter, Debbie, now became the custodial stepmother to two fifteen-year-old boys. With her own son only just reaching puberty, Theresa soon realized that she wasn't totally prepared for the sometimes puzzling and disconcerting behavior of two rambunctious and energetic boys in midadolescence. Her relationship with them was further complicated by the fact that, while Theresa had held a job all her adult life, the twins were used to a full-time, stay-at-home mother.

For the good of George and the twins, Theresa felt she had to maintain civil relations with George's first wife. For the sake of her own children, she maintained a friendly relationship with

Dan and his new wife. She worried about her noncustodial son, Tony, and tried to see him as often as possible. Since it had been agreed that Tony would continue to be raised in his mother's rather than his father's religion, Theresa continued to arrange for the boy's religious education and maintain close contact with all of his teachers.

Theresa's husband, *George*, had the reverse of his new wife's problem; that is, having raised two very independent adolescent boys, he suddenly found himself the stepfather of a rather shy eight-year-old girl. George worried about his relationship with little Debbie, who appeared to have been seriously hurt by her parents' rather stormy divorce. He also tried to establish some sort of relationship with Theresa's son, Tony, on the boy's visits to his mother. Finally, for the sake of his biological children and his stepchildren, he tried to maintain an amiable relationship with his own ex-wife and with Theresa's former husband, Dan.

Roberta, Dan's new wife, had never before been married and had no children of her own. Now, as stepmother to twelve-year-old Tony, she felt not only that she had to work to gain the boy's confidence; she also realized, with a jolt, that she knew very little about the physical and emotional growth stages of childhood and adolescence. She was a complete stranger to the world of PTA and Parents' Nights, and felt awkward in offering advice or imposing discipline on Tony. More and more, Roberta worried about the burden of parenthood. She tried to maintain a friendly and even close relationship with Theresa, in hope that she could learn more about how to deal with the boy.

Then there were the children. Debbie and her twin stepbrothers had to learn to live together as a family, while Debbie and Tony had to learn to live as siblings *apart* from each other. In addition, they found themselves constantly encountering new "aunts," "cousins," and "grandparents." For all of these people life in the stepfamily proved, at least initially, very complicated.

What is missing from the above description is an analysis of the relationships that are perhaps most important and fundamental of all: the relationship between Theresa and George, and that between Dan and Roberta. One might well wonder: With all the emotional complications and needs of new stepfamilies, when do the new spouses get the time and energy to build strong new marriages? Does a stepparent, in effect, have to be a "superparent" and nothing less?

The truth is that stepparenting is not for the timid at heart. Where one or both potential partners already have children, each partner has to form a realistic assessment of his own, his partner's, and the children's emotional needs. Realism, patience, and flexibility are absolutely necessary for the successful and happy stepparent. It is also essential for the potential stepparent to expect, and be content with, less than perfect harmony and devotion in a stepfamily. Love, determination, and above all, a sense of humor are certainly marks of a concerned and successful stepmother or -father.

Anyone deciding to become part of a stepfamily should immediately disabuse himself or herself of unrealistic, overly romantic notions about family life. Despite the existence of one popular television series depicting the endlessly loving, endlessly comic adventures of the various members of an "All-American" stepfamily, the reality is more complicated. In television, all complications and misunderstandings are resolved in an hour or so. Not so for the real-life stepparent.

At the outset, the stepfamily begins its life together facing more potential difficulties than most biological nuclear families. The most obvious and basic difference is that, in the biological nuclear family, the children share, virtually from conception, an intense bond with both spouses. This bond, evident in almost all families, seems to be both biological and psychological in origin and growth.

Indeed, some experts now feel that certain very important emotional aspects of the child-parent relationship have their beginnings in the period before the child is even born. While the entire question of prenatal and immediately postnatal "bonding" between parents and children is still controversial, evidence does seem to be accumulating to suggest that some form of intense parent-infant feelings may be generated during the period of the mother's pregnancy. This bonding would seem to be more obvious, of course, in the case of the biological mother. A woman who desires to bear a child, and who physically and emotionally experiences the growth of that child within her own body, is understandably apt to feel a profound emotional closeness to her newborn infant.

The father who shares, emotionally, each phase of his wife's pregnancy has, after nine months, become acutely aware of his own fathering role. This fathering sense may well be further strengthened by the increasingly common and very healthy practice of allowing men to be present at and to participate in their wives' labor and the delivery of their children.

Furthermore, there is evidence to suggest that mother/infant closeness and cuddling *immediately* after the baby's birth may intensify emotional bonding in both mother and child. Some experts, in fact, posit the existence of a critical period immediately after birth when parent-infant contact takes on particular significance. They feel that physical closeness and cuddling between parent and child during this period greatly enhances the parent-infant relationship as the child develops.

The infant, according to this theory, is more than a passive presence in the bonding process. Aside from the postdelivery experience of physical contact with the mother, it seems that, even in the womb, the infant learns from and reacts to his mother's body and even, to some extent, to the outside world. There is evidence that children in the womb can react to loud noises or even to music. While it is not yet known whether an unborn might acquire certain temperamental or personality characteristics by interacting with its mother's body and her mental states, the possibility is both real and fascinating. If these theories of prenatal development prove to be true, the possible implications are quite important. To take just one such possibility, consider the following: If an infant in the womb can hear and learn to recognize his mother's and father's voices, does it become important for the parents not to argue or express themselves in harsh or angry tones? In other words, can a child, before birth, learn to be frightened — or soothed — by his parents' voices, depending upon the emotional content of those voices?

Biological parents, then, may have had very early experiences of their children (and vice versa) that help to create a natural parent-child bond or relationship. But even if these prenatal or early newborn experiences do not exist, the very fact of the child's birth and life soon establishes the parent-child relationship.

The biological parent raising a young child comes to know that child very well indeed. The attentive young mother — or father — quite simply knows of or has shared every significant event of the child's life and can recite automatically the child's temperamental traits and characteristics, her likes and dislikes. In turn, the child comes very soon to regard her parents as the most important figures in her life. They become for her the ideal, the standard by which all other adults will be judged. What's more, parents and their children share a common history, that conglomeration of small and large tragedies, triumphs, losses, and gains that become the basis of family legend and myth. Those dozens of anecdotes that begin "When you were just a baby . . ." add up to an affectionate family history in which both parents and children play an integral part. This history becomes an important component of the emotional life of the family.

The stepparent however, does not benefit from either the biological or early developmental stages important in forming the parent-child relationship. However young your stepchild may be when you first meet him, he will still be, initially, very much the "little stranger." Thus, the process of coming to know him, and of having him come to know and accept you, may be a rather long and complicated one.

All of this discussion about the biological family is certainly not intended to discourage the stepparent. It is true that the biological parent who lives with his child and who has cared for the child's physical and emotional needs has a natural advantage in gaining the child's love and confidence. It is also true, of course, that some biological parents — whether by reason of their own extreme youth or immaturity, or because of some emotional handicap — are profoundly unable to form the appropriate "parenting" bond with their children.

It is very important for stepparents and prospective stepparents to know that they can, over time, form loving, healthy, satisfying relationships with their stepchildren. With time and understanding, bonds of mutual affection, trust, and intimacy will grow among members of the new family unit. The stepfamily will become a "legitimate entity," with its own ties of family history and love.

Indeed, you only have to look to your own friends to find individuals raised by, and greatly devoted to, their stepparents. David, a businessman in his midthirties, tells a fairly typical story: "My stepfather, whom we called 'Pop' to distinguish him from my biological Dad, married my mother when I was eleven years old. It was hard for my brother and me to get used to having another father, and I guess we weren't too friendly to him at first. But he was real patient with us, never pushing us to show affection for him, never putting down my biological father, whom we used to brag about a lot.

"Eventually, we discovered that Pop had a lot to teach us

— about certain sports, for example, or about the stars — he was an amateur astronomer. We really grew to love him after a while — not as a father, exactly, but as part coach, part uncle, part friend. He was always there for us, in his own way, and he really made a difference."

David is not unusual in his genuine love and respect for his stepfather. And we all know adults who show a similar appreciation for their stepmothers. Carol, a graduate student in her early twenties, described her stepmother with enthusiasm: "'Sue' (we never could bring ourselves to call her 'Mother') married Dad when I was fourteen. She brought her own two younger sons into the house and, for a while, things were pretty tense. I must have had a difficult adolescence or something; anyway, we fought a lot for the first year or two. I resented her taking my Mom's place with Dad, and I had a rough time getting used to those two new 'little brothers.'

"But things calmed down after a while — probably because Sue had the patience of Job and didn't make me feel like a monster after one of my outbursts. After all, all teen-age girls have arguments with their mothers — at least, all my school friends did. Finally I began to realize that, if I'd been living with my own Mom, she and I would probably have arguments, too. Actually, since I only saw my Mom during school vacations, she never tried to discipline me or to set rules. She didn't have to, I guess — Sue did.

"Anyway, Sue never did become my mother, exactly, but she did become my advisor and confidante. It was actually easier for me to talk to her about certain subjects — boys and dates, for example — than it was for me to talk to Mom.

"Also, from Sue I learned a lot about what it means to be a full-time homemaker. Mom was in business; she put in long hours at the office, traveled a lot, things like that. We'd always had housekeepers to help with cooking and cleaning. Until I met Sue, I just didn't think there was anything worthwhile about being 'just' a homemaker. Now I know differently — I have one more option to choose from in my own life."

These two examples illustrate some of the most positive aspects of stepparenting. They also point up one important difference between stepfamilies and biological families.

Stepfathers and stepmothers are not *exactly like* biological fathers and mothers. They are not identical to a child's biological parents; they cannot expect or be expected to fill completely or precisely the role or the void left in the child's life by the absence of the noncustodial biological parent.

It is true that adopted children generally do look on their adoptive parents as "mother" and "father." But this is different from the stepparent situation. For one thing, most children who are adopted are adopted in infancy, a period during which the very earliest parent-child bonds are still being formed. Second, the adopted infant ordinarily has spent very little — if any — time in the care and company of its biological parents. Indeed, in most cases such an infant, before adoption, has not had the experience of any one caretaker who could be singled out as a "parent." Thus, in most cases, the infant's adoptive parents are its first primary caretakers, and the first persons the infant can recognize as mother and father.

It is unusual, however, for a child still in infancy to acquire a stepparent. More commonly, a stepchild, even though he is still a toddler, will have had some significant emotional experience with his biological parents and will know that they are "special" to him in some way. This is true even when the biological parent has literally abandoned the child and lost all contact with him.

So, then, a stepparent is not *exactly* like a biological parent, though he or she may perform all the functions and duties of a biological parent. And a stepchild will not (really, cannot) give a stepparent *exactly* the same type of love, or accord him *exactly* the same emotional significance, as he will give his biological parent.

But this realization should not discourage stepparents. On the contrary, it is a very encouraging and heartening fact. In the past, many stepmothers and stepfathers viewed themselves as failures because they could not replace the biological mother or father in the child's affection. Even today, some stepparents cause themselves unnecessary pain by holding themselves to this impossible — and totally unnecessary — ideal.

Typical of these self-proclaimed "failures" is Arthur, a successful and energetic man in his late thirties. Arthur, who has no biological children, has been married for three years to a woman with two sons, aged nine and twelve. "I'm trying to be a real father to Sam and Jonathan," he announced glumly, "but it's just not working. I know they're not comfortable calling me 'Dad,' so they usually avoid calling me anything at all, except for the occasional 'Hey, you.' And they're always bragging about their natural father, even though the guy's a real bum — a failure in business and in life. To top it all off," Arthur finished angrily, "their natural father doesn't even pay his child-support obligations. I pay all the bills, but the boys just can't appreciate that."

There are many aspects of Arthur's complaint that will be discussed at length below. But it is important to note here that Arthur has, to a large extent, created his own unhappiness. In his own mind, he has set himself up in competition with his stepsons' biological father. Even if Arthur should prove to be a more loving, more skillful, more devoted, and more attractive figure than the biological father, he cannot — and should not — hope to replace that man in his stepsons' eyes. Sam and Jonathan know very well that they have only one biological father. No matter what that father's real or imagined shortcomings, his sons have a normal, healthy need to "look up" to him.

If Arthur would acknowledge to himself and his new family that he is not a father, but a *stepfather*, he might well find himself able to relax and enjoy the affection of his stepsons.

The word *stepparent* does not mean "second-rate" or "inferior to the biological parent." Rather, it means only that, while stepchildren may love a stepparent very intensely, they will love him *differently* from the way they love their biological parent. A stepparent can play an important — indeed, a critical — role in a child's emotional life. He can be valued and loved *as a stepparent*. He need not compete with the biological parent for a child's love; an emotionally healthy child has enough love to go around.

If the stepparent cannot expect to be loved in exactly the same way as the biological parent, what can he realistically expect? There is no one answer to this important question; there is no single correct relationship between stepparent and stepchild.

It may be helpful, in this respect, to turn back and reread the stories of those two now-grown stepchildren, David and Carol. David, with great fondness, described his stepfather as "part coach, part uncle, part friend." And Carol, with equal affection, seemed to view her stepmother as part mother, part role model, part "older sister" confidante and advisor.

Both David and Carol sought, and received, from their stepparents those qualities that met their individual emotional needs. These needs will vary considerably from one child to another and, in any one child, from one developmental stage to another.

David's and Carol's stepparents both behaved, perhaps instinctively, in a very healthy and positive way. They did not immediately impose themselves on their new stepchildren and demand to be accepted and loved as parents. Instead, they quietly allowed themselves an introductory period with the stepchild, so that the child could adjust to their presence in the home. They also recognized that it is quite common for stepchildren to re-

sent the stepparent at first, and they did not retaliate or get overly upset when the stepchild displayed this anger and resentment
through arguments and tantrums.

Most important, the stepparents here allowed themselves time
to get to know the children without placing any demands or expectations on them. When they became more familiar with the
interests and emotional needs of their new stepchildren, they
were able to approach them in a helpful and nonthreatening
manner.

For example, David's Pop (who understood the boy's need to
distinguish him from his biological father) discovered David's
interest in sports. Since he had been a serious athlete himself as
a boy, Pop began to coach David in his favorite sports. By helping the boy in this and similar ways, David's stepfather allowed
the natural, unforced growth of a relationship built on affection
and respect.

Carol's stepmother, Sue, acted in a similar fashion. Recognizing
that Carol was experiencing a stage in her adolescence where
she had to test her own attitudes and opinions by pitting herself against a strong female role model, Sue was careful not to
overreact when Carol deliberately tried to provoke arguments
with her. She remained firm in her own opinions, but dealt with
Carol's outbursts matter-of-factly, refusing to respond with rage
or hysteria. Carol, in turn, soon began to realize that Sue did not
regard her as a "bad" person, but respected her moods and feelings. Eventually, Carol came to return Sue's affection and respect
and found in her a confidante who was emotionally close enough
— and just distant enough — to help her with her most troubling
adolescent secrets.

In both of these instances, the stepparent exercised considerable patience and restraint during what can be a very difficult
trial period for new stepfamilies. They accepted that their new
stepchildren might well go through a period of being tense, un-

comfortable, distant, or even hostile to them. These stepparents realized that such negative feelings were, for the children, an almost inevitable part of their adjustment to a new family situation. They knew that these initial displays of coldness, or anger, were not really a comment on their individual qualities as stepparents, or as human beings.

Also, neither Pop nor Sue tried to impose themselves on their new stepchildren as a substitute for the children's own mother or father. Instead, they wisely allowed themselves time to get to know them, and then offered their affection and help in ways that the children could accept and appreciate.

You will notice that, in describing these two very successful stepparents, we have used the word "patience" more than once. Men and women who are considering taking on the stepparent role must realize, at the outset, that they will be called on to exercise a very great deal of patience with their new stepchildren. We will discuss below, in detail, some of the particular problems and adjustments that the stepfamily will encounter in the first phases of their life together. But we should note here that the period of adjustment may turn out to be longer than either stepparent or stepchild would have expected.

Exactly how long *is* "longer than expected"? At a minimum, the stepfamily should expect that at least a year will elapse before the family members learn to function together comfortably, as a unit. It is more likely to be two or three years before the stepfamily really feels itself to be a cohesive "family." Of course, this will vary from family to family. There is no one timetable for the healthy emotional development of a stepfamily. The important point here is that you should not attempt to force the pace of developing family relationships. Neither should you feel like a failure if your stepfamily fails to develop according to some arbitrary timetable.

If all of this begins to sound impossibly difficult, take heart.

When we say that a stepfamily may take two or three years to learn how to function as a family, we don't mean to imply that things need be genuinely unpleasant during that entire period. Indeed, any obvious or major problems are apt to surface quite early in the stepfamily's life together. These problems will demand immediate attention and some sort of relatively prompt resolution.

But it takes longer for the complex organism we call a stepfamily to settle into its own emotional rhythm, its own unique style of being together. Finding this style can be an exciting and satisfying endeavor, even if it takes a year or two.

Besides a surfeit of patience, the new stepparent would do well to cultivate another basic quality: a lively sense of humor. Humor helps put difficult moments into perspective. The ability to laugh at one's situation, and at oneself, is one component of a very healthy survival instinct. Consider Emily, a thirty-three-year-old lawyer, never before married, whose marriage made her the stepmother of two boys, aged six and nine, and a ten-year-old girl:

"I really thought at first that I was in over my head," Emily later confessed. "Even though we had a part-time housekeeper, I wanted to be available to mother the kids in the evenings and on weekends. And almost immediately Gil's [her husband's] business started to pick up and suddenly he was out of town a lot, on business.

"I liked the kids. After all, I'd known them for almost a year before we were married, and we'd gotten along fine. But I soon realized that being a stepmother was different from being a visitor.

"It started out as a disaster. For one thing, I couldn't cook. Never tried. Didn't know much about keeping house, either. Most important, I realized — too late — that I really didn't know the first thing about raising kids!

"Things rapidly got worse. The kids, who absolutely adored

me when I was just Daddy's friend, began to find fault with everything I did. Nothing about me — my cooking, my work, not even my hairdo — was as good as their real Mommy's was.

"After about six or eight nerve-wracking weeks of this, my sense of the ridiculous finally got the better of me. Looking back, I'm surprised it took that long. I've always used humor as a 'safety valve' whenever I'm under extra pressure at the office, or during a particularly nerve-wracking trial.

"Anyway, I suddenly began to find everything very silly, and I found myself laughing a lot — at my own culinary failures, at the kids' constant complaining, at my misunderstandings with the housekeeper. The whole situation reminded me of some sitcom you might see on television.

"The funny thing was, the more humor I saw in things, the less frightening everything seemed. The kids began to laugh with me, rather than argue with me. They even began to laugh at their own grumblings, so that the whole thing became kind of a joke.

"After that, we all seemed to relax a bit. We still had plenty of problems to work out, but a lot of the tension seemed to evaporate."

Emily, in this case, instinctively hit upon one of the most useful coping mechanisms any stepparent can have: humor. It would be shallow and just plain wrong to assume that you can literally laugh your troubles away. Problems do not disappear simply because you can joke about them; they need to be worked out with sincerity, openness, and a willingness to communicate with other family members. But the importance of a healthy sense of humor cannot be underestimated. The ability to laugh at yourself, and at your situation, gives you a sense of perspective that makes it easier to abort the ups and downs of any difficult period. Humor allows you to relax; it staves off the painful anxiety that comes from seeing yourself as overwhelmed by a new and complicated living situation.

A sense of humor is also, as Emily put it, a real safety valve;

it can be used to express what are essentially angry or frustrated feelings in a gentle, nonthreatening way. In Emily's case, she was able to joke with her stepchildren in such a way that they came to see that their own constant complaining was unfair, even funny. The children thus gained some insight into and some perspective on their own behavior toward their stepmother.

Though Emily did find a way to cope with the many unexpected complications she had found in stepparenting, she might have avoided some of the problems altogether by preparing herself and the children even before her marriage. After all, at some point in her dating relationship with Gil both of them must have acknowledged that marriage was a strong possibility. At that point, both Emily and Gil should have started to consider the most natural way for Emily and the children to develop a friendly, positive relationship.

When divorced parents remarry, the resulting new families and stepfamilies can include an incredibly broad spectrum of new relationships involving biological parents, their children, their new spouses, their stepchildren — not to mention the ex-spouses' new spouses, and aunts, uncles, grandparents, and so forth. The most important of these new relationships are those involving stepparents and children, those involving new spouses, and the relationships between stepbrothers and stepsisters. Let's examine these new categories of stepfamily relationship separately.

In the preceding chapter we discussed certain emotional and psychological developments that might be expected to affect the new stepparent and stepchild in the period of parental courtship, marriage, and initial family adjustments. There are, however, other perfectly normal emotional states or events that will affect the development of the stepfamily unit. A familiarity with and acceptance of these almost inevitable complications can greatly ease the stepfamily through the rite of passage of its first few years.

The new stepparent must keep in mind that his stepson or stepdaughter is a child of divorce. Even though the divorce may have become final years earlier, it will quite likely have left the child with certain attitudes, fears, or unresolved conflicts. This may be true even when the child appears to be perfectly accepting of his changed life.

We are not talking here about serious emotional or behavioral changes, which call for professional counseling. But divorce is certainly a traumatic event for a child. He may have underlying feelings and pain that certain new events may reawaken. The event most likely to stir up these feelings is the remarriage of a parent.

The most sensitive issue that will arise between stepparent and child concerns the child's relationship with his noncustodial biological parent — the parent whose place is now filled, in the child's home, by the new stepparent. The presence of a stepparent, and perhaps also of stepbrothers and sisters, in the child's household means that the child will have to find a new definition of the idea of "family." In redefining his family, the child will have to find a way to love and accept these important new people, while retaining his love and loyalty to his biological family members. This is not an easy task, even for an adult. For a child, it is especially difficult.

The new family — the new stepparent and his spouse — can make it easier for the child to resolve his resentment and conflict of loyalties, once they understand the child's predicament. We have already seen some ways in which this can be done — by not forcing the child to address the stepparent as a parent, for example. Adults who respond harshly to the child's behavior aggravate the situation.

After his mother's remarriage, nine-year-old Greg behaved coolly toward his new stepfather. At the same time, he began to talk incessantly about his biological father, boasting about the father's success, his athletic skills, his achievements in business. While Greg was not rude to his stepfather, Matthew, he rarely seemed to appreciate Matthew's efforts to form a friendship with him. When Matthew took the boy to a film or sport event or bought him a gift, Greg's "thank you" always sounded halfhearted. After a while, Greg's seeming adoration for his biological father angered both Matthew and Becky, Greg's mother.

"It was not just unfair," Becky complained. "It was absolutely ludicrous. The truth was that Bob (Greg's biological father) is an acute alcoholic, who ruined his career and our marriage. I don't even know where he's living now. He's come to visit Greg exactly three times since our divorce two years ago, even though he has weekly visitation rights.

"Not only that. Bob's never paid the child support the court ordered — never even discussed it with me. Matthew pays all the bills without any complaint.

"One evening at dinner, when Greg was going on and on about the fun he used to have with his father, Matthew blew up. I should mention that this was the same day Matthew took the afternoon off from work to take Greg to the circus. Matthew said it was high time that Greg knew the truth about his father. He told Greg about Bob's drinking, his failures, his insensitivity in visiting his own child. He talked about the missing child-support payments. He said that Bob was a drunk, a bum who didn't care about his own children.

"To tell the truth, I was glad that all this was coming out in the open. I told Greg, very calmly, that what Matthew had said was true, and I mentioned how disappointed I'd been in Bob. I reminded Greg of how good Matthew had been to him.

"I really wasn't prepared, though, for Greg's reaction to all this. I thought he might have a tantrum, or be upset for a little while. But it's been almost a month, and he's so quiet and withdrawn that it frightens me."

"What puzzles me most is that none of what Matthew said about Bob could have come as a surprise to Greg. After all, before the divorce he saw his father drunk every single night. He used to cry about it. He certainly knew that Bob didn't come to see him after the divorce. And, while I'd never told him about the child-support money, I think he's smart enough to have figured that out for himself, a long time ago."

It's easy to understand Matthew's resentment over Greg's unappreciative, distant attitude. It's also easy to understand Becky's anxiety to have Greg understand the truth, so that the new family could develop loving relationships of its own. Still, their method of forcing Greg to confront the truth was harmful, and brought unnecessary pain to the boy. It served not only to destroy the boy's fantasy that his biological father was a special person who loved his son, but it also made Greg feel that he was being forced to abandon his father, and forced to transfer his love to Matthew.

Children of divorce almost always idealize the noncustodial parent. This may partly be due to the fact that the child feels guilty about not living with that parent and allowing another adult to assume the parent's role. If the child feels guilty about abandoning a parent, or trading him for another, he might allay these guilt feelings by praising that parent at every opportunity.

There is also, of course, the fact that the noncustodial parent, who sees the child only for brief periods, often plays the role of the "good-time" parent. Parents who miss their children's company and feel guilty about not living with them tend to overcompensate by indulging the children when they *can* visit. This is not, as we've noted earlier, the most productive way for a noncustodial parent and his child to spend their time together.

But it's commonly done nonetheless. Every visitation becomes a party, in the child's eyes. Endless entertainment, junk food, a complete absence of rules or discipline — these are some of the ways certain parents try to show their love during visitation days.

The custodial parent and stepparent simply cannot indulge the child this way. Things such as a proper diet, household chores, supervised homework sessions, curfews — these are a necessary part of the child's ordinary, everyday life. But what child would not be tempted to idolize the parent who threw all these rules away? The everyday job of raising children is not always easy for either parent or child.

Finally, children, unless they are seriously insecure, come to take their custodial family somewhat for granted. They see them every day; they accept that the custodial family is responsible for their physical and emotional welfare. And it is a common human trait not to acknowledge the importance and value of what we have come to take for granted.

In the case of Greg's family, his mother's statement was exactly right: The boy *did* know that his father had a drinking problem, was unhappy about his father's neglect of him, and did at least suspect that his father was not meeting his child-support payments. Even so, Greg had some fond memories of his father and still loved him. But he also felt growing affection for his stepfather, Matthew. Greg's guilt over loving his new father over his old led him to his constant praise of Bob. By exaggerating his biological father's virtues, he felt less like a traitor.

It is important that stepparents recognize the reasons for the child's idealization of his noncustodial parent. The child is not being difficult or ungrateful; he *needs* to think and talk this way about the absent parent. This is an essential part of development in the child's conception of family; it is a stage that, ideally, will eventually allow the child to achieve a more balanced, truthful acceptance of both biological parent and stepparent.

One other fact that stepparents should be aware of is that a healthy child, a secure, loved child, is not by nature a grateful being. Occasionally, adults who are not used to dealing with children will talk about how ungrateful or selfish children are; such adults become hurt or angry when their gifts or treats are received with apparent indifference.

The truth is, that children are not ungrateful for the care and the gifts they receive from adults; rather, having been cared for all of their young lives, they simply do not look on most acts of kindness, or on most gifts, as a true surprise.

After all, the child has been physically helpless, to one degree or another, since birth. He has been cared for all of his life; he assumes that being cared for and being the object of adult attention are all in the normal scheme of things. And the normal scheme of things does not merit thanks, or gratitude.

In fact, the child who shows an *inordinate* degree of surprise or appreciation when he is shown loving attention may well be an insecure, unhappy child. The normal well-cared-for child takes his physical nurturance and comfort for granted. The child who displays inordinate surprise or gratitude for "being taken care of" may well have a history of physical or emotional neglect.

This does not mean that a child should not be taught to say "thank you" where thanks are appropriate. The ritual, repeated in millions of homes, of having your little boy or girl sit down and write "thank you notes" after receiving gifts or favors is an important step in teaching the child about generosity and gratitude.

Where does this leave the stepparent, now living with children whom he or she not only supports financially, but who supplies their daily needs and deals with their daily crises?

It is frustrating to be taken for granted and to have the superior virtues of the noncustodial parent constantly thrown up to you. However, the worst thing you can do under these trying circumstances is to criticize the child's hero, the noncustodial parent who, apparently, can do no wrong in the child's eyes.

The steppparent's criticism will not only fail to change the child's feelings toward his biological parent; it will also hamper the growth of an affectionate relationship between the complaining stepparent and the child. This sort of criticism, however true, is bound to be met with either resentment or guilt feelings on the child's part.

The stepparent's attitude toward the absent biological parent should always be one of respect. This is true regardless of whatever secret resentment, jealousy, or hostility the stepparent feels, justified or not. This does *not* mean that the stepparents must wax ecstatic about the biological parent at every opportunity. It does mean not to ridicule or criticize the biological parent when the child is present.

When the child asks the stepparent, "What do you think of my father [or mother]?" the response, delivered in what should be a pleasant tone of voice, may be fairly neutral: "I don't know him very well, but I know that you love him very much. He must be a very fine man for you to love him, and I know that he loves you, too."

This neutral or somewhat positive attitude helps ease two problems. First of all, it spares the child the conflict of loyalties discussed above; the child now knows he has the stepparent's approval to continue his loving relationship with his biological parent.

Avoiding hostility toward the child's noncustodial parent has another — very practical — benefit. Assuming that the child keeps in touch with his absent parent, as most do, there are bound to be occasions when stepparent and noncustodial parent are in contact. These occasions may be as simple as greeting the parent when he comes to call for the child on visitation day; they may be as important as conferring with the biological parent when the child is ill or has a learning problem in school. For the child's sake, these problems will be resolved more easily and completely if all adult parties — biological parents and stepparents — are on civil terms. No one expects a newly married man or woman to make a best friend out of his or her new partner's ex-spouse; that is the stuff of which only movies marketed as "sophisticated comedies" are made. These relationships may be as formal as you choose; it is necessary only to be able to discuss matters without rancor, where the child is concerned.

Another way in which the stepparent can help the stepfamily unit to grow together into a "family" is by acknowledging an obvious fact, that is, the stepparent's new spouse, the biological parent, naturally enjoys a more intense and critical relationship with the child than the stepparent will ever have. Indeed, it would be worrisome if this were *not* true. The biological parent, present from the child's birth, bound to the child by ties of love and blood, feels a unique bond to his or her child. The child, of course, feels the same specialness in his relationship with his biological mother or father.

The stepparent must be generous in acknowledging that bond. Too often, the new stepparent fears that he will not be considered to be "as good as" the biological parent. He may feel threatened or angered by the child's special displays of love for the biological parent.

But the stepparent must understand and accept the fact that his spouse will always have a "special relationship" with his stepchild. In fact, he should indicate his approval of this special love by acknowledging that the two — biological parent and child — should have some special time set aside so that they can be together, without the distraction or interruptions of other adults and children.

It is very much to the stepparent's — and the entire stepfamily's — advantage to encourage these special times when biological parent and child can spend a few hours or even a day together. It's not necessary to have formal activities planned for this time. It might be a special treat for parent and child to spend an afternoon at the park or at a movie. But the main purpose of these periods is merely to allow parent and child to have each other's complete attention, if only for a little while.

These special times — whether it be an hour before each bedtime, or the whole of a weekend day — allow the child the opportunity to voice fears or apprehensions, to discuss his feelings about school, his friends, and above all, to talk about his family. For these hours, he can be confident that the parent is all ears.

The stepparent, too, benefits greatly from these periods of special closeness between his spouse and his stepchild. For one thing, this time together reinforces the child's belief that he will always be "special" to his biological parent. All healthy, secure children need to be sure of their special place in the parent's affection.

When the relationship between biological parent and child remains firm and secure, the stepparent also benefits. The emotionally secure child will not feel that he has to compete with the stepparent for his parent's love and attention; he knows that he is loved. Such a child will not have to learn to resent the new adult who has "stolen" his parent's attention. He does not have to compete with the stepparent for the parent's love; he knows that there is plenty to go around.

Also, the child who knows that he deserves, and will get, a special time to be alone with his parent, a time to share his intimate fears and hopes with the parent, is more likely to accept the stepparent's need to have some private time with his new spouse. David and Martha, a newly married couple who each brought one child to the marriage, made this happy discovery only a few weeks into their marriage.

"When we finally set up a household," David recounted later, "we were incredibly anxious to establish ourselves as a real family. I guess both Martha and I, in the back of our minds, had this terrible fear that the stepfamily thing just wouldn't work out.

"Up till then, it had been O.K. Before the wedding I'd been taking my Ellen, who was just five, over to Martha's and we'd pretty much spend the whole weekend there. Sean was only six, so we thought that he and Ellen would make terrific playmates. And they did, apart from the usual fights kids get into.

"Martha and I had decided we'd act like a real family; she'd treat Ellen as if she were her own and I'd act the same way with Sean. We didn't give our own kids any special time, or any special treatment.

"It just didn't work. I told Ellen that Sean was my real child, too, and Martha told Sean the same. We thought it would relax things, make them feel secure with both of us.

"So we did everything together; we shared all our time. But the kids didn't seem to like it. There were arguments and constant tension; Sean started to whine and cling to Martha; Ellen did the same to me. It was very upsetting; we felt less like a family than we had before the wedding."

Martha and David discussed the problem and realized that before their marriage each, being a single parent, had spent substantial time in the exclusive company of his own child. Sean was used to having a great deal of time alone with Martha, as Ellen was with David.

Once David and Ellen stopped the pretense that they were all one big happy family, the emotional climate improved enormously. Both parents created a time to be alone with their biological child, as they had been almost continuously in the past. When the children realized that they had retained the special love and interest of the biological parent, much of the tension in the family household slowly evaporated. Only then could stepbrother and stepsister begin, with confidence, to establish their own friendship within the framework of the new family.

There is one other area that is an important issue in the relationship of some new stepparents to some stepchildren. It is an area widely misunderstood and not often discussed. The conventional wisdom, which is utterly incorrect, states that the feelings we are about to discuss are not even experienced by "decent" people. The truth is otherwise, and I believe that we must be aware of that truth in order to control potentially harmful or destructive behavior.

The area concerns sexual feelings: in this case, sexual feelings felt by the new stepparent toward the adolescent stepchild. This topic has long been taboo; parents, stepparents, even mental-health professionals have historically been reluctant to discuss sexual feelings felt by an adult toward a child or adolescent. Words like "twisted," "perverted" and "pathological" were routinely used whenever the subject was approached.

I believe that this attitude is partly due to a misunderstanding of the difference between sexual feelings or impulses, which all adults feel, and the acting out of truly pathological behavior, as in the sexual molestation of children.

We are not talking here about adults who actually engage in overt sexual behavior, either consenting or nonconsenting, with children, a type of activity that is tremendously harmful to the child. It can gravely harm personality development in the child. It can engender strong feelings of guilt and revulsion that may render impossible the later development of loving, adult, sexual relationships.

Sexual activity between parent and child is called, of course, incest. Sexual activity between stepparent and child is not, technically speaking, incest. But it is pathological and destructive to the child, nonetheless. I cannot emphasize strongly enough the damage that parent-child sexual activity can do to a child. Such activity is, statistically speaking, most commonly performed by the male parent with the female child. Any adult engaged in such behavior should seek immediate professional help. Certainly, a child who has been victimized in this fashion should have expert professional help.

It is not the aim of this book to detail the horrors of sexual behavior carried out by adults on children and stepchildren. But we should emphasize, again, that such actions are in no way normal and cannot be condoned. However, the experience of having sexual *feelings* or *thoughts* toward adolescents in one's own family is *not* pathological, unless those feelings are acted upon with children. Sexual *feelings* are neutral. Feelings alone can neither hurt nor harm another person.

We have all had feelings or impulses of which we are not proud. A recent President once confessed that he had "lusted in his heart" after many women, though he was happily married. And which of us, rudely cut off in the middle of a traffic jam, has not imagined doing physical violence to the offending driver?

Sexual feelings are a natural part of every healthy adult's emotional make-up. Most people who have well-adjusted and tolerant attitudes toward sexual behavior — their own or other people's — would still feel shocked or repelled if confronted with sexual feelings toward any child, let alone their own child. Many adults assume that such sexual feelings would lead to overt, destructive behavior.

To avoid that kind of destructive sexual behavior, psychologically healthy adults and growing children make use of a nearly universal, crucially important psychological mechanism: the "incest taboo." A forty-year-old man, for example, may well find a seventeen-year-old girl sexually attractive. But what if that attractive seventeen-year-old is his own daughter? This is where the incest taboo enters into family life, protecting both father and daughter from experiencing or encouraging sexual feelings toward each other. The incest taboo is a part of the family's psychological life from the very beginning of the parent-child relationship. As we discussed earlier, most fathers allow themselves less physical contact with their infant daughters than they do with their infant sons. Mothers, in turn, have less intimate physical contact with infant sons than they do with daughters. As the opposite-sex child grows older, physical contact with the parent changes in both frequency and quality. This happens gradually and almost automatically. There is a point, for example, when a father begins to feel that his daughter is "too big" and "too old" to clamber up onto his lap. A mother's kisses and caresses for her growing son become more formal, more removed.

The child, too, as he becomes more aware of his developing sexuality, demands more privacy and more formal physical contact. The opposite-sex parent is asked not to enter the bathroom when the child is bathing; bedroom doors are suddenly closed when the child is getting dressed. The adolescent, during puberty, becomes extremely aware of himself as a sexual being. Modesty becomes important in the home; bedroom doors are more often closed. Often, the teen-ager becomes laconic, or even secretive, about his emotional and social life.

We see, then, that the incest taboo develops over a long period of time. We are not always aware of it, of course. But, in the biological family, the combination of shared history and sense of "blood ties" almost always prevents family members from allowing themselves to experience sexual feelings toward one another.

But where does this leave the stepparent, who shares with his stepchildren, at the outset, no mutual history and no blood ties?

Adults do not, ordinarily, look upon small children as sexually attractive beings. But certain adolescents, especially the more mature-looking among them, can appear sexually attractive in the eyes of many adults. And, in some cases, new stepparents may be astonished and horrified to discover that they do entertain sexual feelings toward their own stepchild.

It does no good to feel guilty about having sexual thoughts or feelings themselves; these things are simply not under the control of our conscious minds. It is, however, absolutely essential that the stepparent examine why and how these feelings came about. Very often, such an examination will reveal certain circumstances that encourage sexual feelings toward the stepchild.

The stepparent who is troubled by such feelings should studiously avoid all situations in the home that could be considered provocative. He or she should not remain in the room when the stepchild is dressing. The stepparent should not in any way encourage flirtatious behavior. He or she should not overpraise the stepchild's physical attributes or appearance. The stepparent should make an effort to be particularly sensitive to occasions where he or she may be tempted to behave in a flirtatious or inappropriately adult way with the stepchild.

Sexual feelings or fantasies do not always exist only in the stepparent's mind. Occasionally, the adolescent stepchild himself will wittingly or unwittingly encourage the stepparent's sexual attention. The psychological reasons for this behavior are usually found in the child's previous experience of abandonment. Compulsive and inappropriate sexual behavior in adolescents is often rooted in the child's history of emotional neglect. In such cases, the child learns that attention can be bought with sex; the classic promiscuous girl or boy is often one who feels that he or she cannot find love in any other way.

It is not necessary to dwell on this problem of sexual feelings between stepparent and child. There are, however, a few guidelines the stepparent can use if he or she finds that there are sexual implications to the stepparent's relationship with the child. The most important consideration is to avoid situations that may seem unduly intimate or provocative. Thus, as we noted above, stepparents should not encourage adolescent stepchildren of the opposite sex to undress before them. Any other activity, such as certain forms of physical affection, that makes the stepparent uncomfortable should also be avoided.

Occasionally, as noted, the impetus for flirtatious or provocative behavior will seem to come from the stepchild. If the stepparent, after studying the situation, is satisfied that this is the case, he or she may also reasonably conclude that the stepchild is somehow emotionally troubled.

If the stepchild's seductive behavior continues, despite the stepparent's best efforts to discourage it, then either stepparent or stepchild, or possibly both, are in need of professional counseling. A stepfamily cannot hope to function as a healthy and loving family where these destructive tensions are dominant. It is best, at this point, to seek professional guidance so that the emotional future of the family may be saved.

Another "new" relationship that is of paramount importance to the stepfamily is the most obvious yet least discussed relationship: that of the newly married couple, husband and wife, biological parent and stepparent.

The adjustments that this newly married couple will make mirror the adjustments of all new spouses. The added considerations are, of course, those that come from the extra responsibilities of stepparenting. These responsibilities, or a sample of them, were outlined in some detail in the previous chapter. Generally speaking, however, the "extra" attributes of this new husband and wife, one or both of whom may be stepparents, may be summed up in a single word: *generosity*.

Generosity. This means different things, in the context of the stepfamily.

The stepparent, for example, should accept the fact that the welfare of his stepchildren changes, to some extent, the emotional shape of the conventional new marriage. For one thing, the new stepparent must accept, as a continuing presence in his life, the pressures of his stepchild's other biological parent, his spouse's ex-husband or wife.

We have discussed at some length the stepchild's need to maintain a closeness and special loyalty to his noncustodial parent. This is not always possible, of course, since the noncustodial parent sometimes removes himself, physically or geographically, from the child's life. Where that parent is both accessible and interested in the child's welfare, however, the stepparent should do all he can to encourage the relationship between biological parent and child.

This means, inevitably, that the stepparent must be willing to accept the existence of a continuing relationship between his new spouse and her ex-spouse. If the child's welfare is truly the paramount consideration, then it is only a matter of common sense that both biological parents will share an interest, exchange important information, and discuss the child's progress or problems with one another. To the newly married man or woman, the stepchild's problems may become a source of concern for very different reasons.

Mark, newly married to Brenda, the mother of three boys, felt some initial resentment and jealousy in this respect. "Of course I expected that Brenda and Tim [the boys' father] would be in touch when something came up concerning the kids," he recounted, "but I guess I never stopped to think just what form that communication would take.

"As it turned out, Brenda and Tim had been having dinner together about once a month just to exchange information about the kids. Then the custody order was exchanged; instead of the boys living with us all the time Brenda and Tim arranged joint custody.

"After that it seemed like those two were together all the time:

on the phone, meeting for coffee. When six-year-old Billy started having problems with asthma, they talked constantly, discussing doctors, treatments — everything. It just seemed kind of, well, intimate to me, as if they had a secret. I really started to feel jealous, though intellectually I knew jealousy was perfectly baseless."

Fortunately, Mark was able to discuss his feelings with Brenda, and the two of them came to see each other's point of view. Mark accepted the fact that his wife's meetings with Tim *were* necessary, in view of their son's serious health problem. Brenda, for her part, began to see why Mark was feeling jealous and left out. She took more care to make Mark aware of and a part of Billy's medical treatment. When an important event or decision occurred — Billy's approaching hospitalization, for example — all three adults met and participated in making decisions about the boy's care.

This example, incidentally, illustrates another important consideration in the relationship between new couples, when one is a biological parent and one a stepparent. That is, the biological parent must make it clear — to himself, his spouse, and his children — that the stepparent has legitimate authority in the home. Otherwise, the stepfamily can never become a workable family unit.

One new stepmother, Rochelle, encountered this problem very early in her marriage to David. While David's wife had custody of the twelve-year-old daughter, Diane, the girl was allowed to spend most weekends and every summer vacation in her father's home. Before her marriage, Rochelle had gotten on very well with Diane; afterward, things changed abruptly.

Rochelle relates: "Before David and I were married, everything was fine between Diane and me. But I'd never stopped to think that there was an important difference, in her eyes, between my being Daddy's girl friend and my being a stepmother.

"I didn't move into David's home until after we were married; then the trouble began. I hadn't realized what a mess a young girl can make out of a house in one weekend. She simply refused to clean up after herself — wash dishes, pick up her room, or do anything else. Now, I admit I might be too concerned with neatness, but believe me — by Sunday night Diane always left our house looking like the wrath of God. And since I stayed home during the week, while David worked, I'd spend every Monday cleaning up after Diane.

"What hurt me most, though, was David's attitude. He never backed me up when I gave the girl a direction, or even made a request. If I asked her to do the dishes, or told her not to hang on the phone all day, she'd go to him. He'd always sabotage my authority. Then Diane would pay me even less attention. 'Daddy says I don't have to do that,' she'd say. It began to drive me crazy. I came to dread the girl's visits, and I found myself getting really angry with David."

In fact, David was creating an impossible situation for his new wife, by making it clear to Diane that she need not pay any attention to her new stepmother's authority. This kind of behavior on the biological parent's part can create enormous tension between spouses, and render the life of the stepfamily as a whole totally unworkable.

The stepparent should be an adult authority figure to the family's children. If the parent and stepparent have very different ideas about how that authority should be exercised, and about how children should be taught to act, they must reach an agreement on these important issues. Ideally, these things should be discussed and agreed upon before the marriage. In any event, they should be discussed out of the children's hearing. Otherwise, the children may come to feel that they are both participants and pawns in the couple's battle of wills.

There are a few reasons why some biological parents, like

David, refuse to acknowledge their spouse's authority over the children. In this case David might have felt guilty about the fact that he had become a part-time noncustodial father. These guilt feelings may have made him reluctant to impose any discipline on Diane when she was able to visit him.

Sometimes, too, biological parents actually feel resentment over the stepparent's attempts to assert ownership over their stepchildren. This resentment is very often irrational, and indicates a deeper tension within the husband-wife relationship.

Other hidden stresses, too, may interfere with the newly married couple's relationship. As an example, consider the newly married couple in which both husband and wife have children from previous marriages. Often, only one spouse will have custody of his or her children, and, even today, that spouse is most likely to be the new wife. But in any case, this situation may leave one spouse in a household where he or she lives with stepchildren, while his or her biological or own children live with an ex-spouse.

Commonly, this living arrangement may produce subconscious feelings of guilt and anger. The stepparent may feel resentful that he can spend more time with his stepchildren than he is allowed to spend with his biological children. These submerged feelings may be deflected toward the stepchildren or toward his new spouse. The stepparent may find himself arguing constantly with his spouse over the stepchildren's behavior or habits. Or he may find himself developing a sudden dislike for a stepchild for whom he had always previously felt affection.

Feelings of resentment, competition, anxiety, inadequacy, anger are most dangerous to family life when they remain hidden, or deliberately censored by the parent or stepparents. The stepfamily situation is, after all, an emotionally complicated one, particularly when *both* new spouses have biological children. There are many people in this family drama who must rather quickly become "family," even though they may have been, until recently, complete or comparative strangers.

The key to working out these problems and conflicted feelings lies in that overused but important word: *communication*. Any couple entering into a marriage that involves stepparenting should agree, at the outset, to be particularly honest and open with each other. No matter how embarrassed a spouse may be about harboring angry or negative thoughts about members of the stepfamily, these feelings must be examined and discussed. This promise of honesty is of primary importance to the life of the family. It is more easily made, of course, if husband and wife also agree beforehand to listen to negative feelings and react lovingly and dispassionately, rather than with a knee-jerk reflex of anger and rejection.

One final word should be said about a certain type of stepparent: the homosexual stepparent. There are, and have always been, marriages that end partly because one spouse decides his sexual preference is homosexual rather than heterosexual. And though the law in this area is far from settled, a significant minority of custody suits have been won by the homosexual biological parent. In many of these cases, the homosexual parent has set up a long-term or permanent relationship with a lover, and the two share a household.

Even if custody is denied the homosexual parent, it is almost certain that the noncustodial parent will have visitation rights with the child. In most cases, this means that the child will stay at the home of the homosexual couple during weekends or holidays. In such cases both biological parents, custodial and noncustodial, have posed the question: What is the proper role of the homosexual parent's partner in the child's life?

The best answer is that, in a stable adult homosexual or heterosexual relationship, where the two adults are living together, the nonparent partner does in effect become a "stepparent" to the child. This seems the most consistent and least confusing solution for both child and adults. The homosexual partner should be an adult authority figure for the child when that child is in the parent's household.

Any child, sooner or later, will discover the nature of a homosexual parent's relationship with his lover. How one or both parents choose to explain that relationship is for the involved individuals to decide, as we noted in chapter 2. It would seem, however, that an honest, nonjudgmental explanation would be best for both parent and child.

Another situation with which the new stepfamily must learn to cope concerns the relationship between stepbrothers, and -sisters (stepsiblings). For children, who do not have the sophisticated intellect and emotional resources of adults, this adjustment may be the most difficult of all.

Stepbrothers and -sisters may well feel crowded on two fronts, for they must find emotional *and* physical space to accommodate their new siblings. In the usual situation, one biological parent will move, with his children, into the spouse's existing home. This fact alone is apt to make stepsiblings feel crowded. Unless the family lives in an extremely large house, children may have to double up on bedrooms. The child who is accustomed to the psychological pleasure of having his own bedroom may suddenly find it invaded by another child whom he barely knows, and whom he certainly has not had time to grow to love. We already know that relatively small changes in a child's environment may make a very large difference to the child. Sharing space with a new brother or sister will be seen by the child as an enormous adjustment.

Just as important, or more so, is the emotional adjustment the child must make to "sharing" his biological parent with the new stepsiblings. Our discussion of stepparent-stepchild adjustment in the previous chapter should make it clear that, for the child, learning to share his parent with the parent's new spouse is hard enough. What loving child wants to compete for his parent's attention with ready-made rivals who are his own age?

As you might expect, a new home full of stepsiblings is bound to experience some conflict. Even children who are the best of friends find the occasion to quarrel; new stepbrothers and sisters are apt to find many more such occasions. This is more true the closer stepbrothers and -sisters are in age. Where age difference is relatively great (say between a fifteen-year-old and his three-year-old stepsister) the open conflict will probably be lessened.

When fights do occur between stepsiblings, they are usually over concrete things: territory (as in a shared bedroom), toys, other possessions. The best thing for stepparents to do, at least in the early stages, is not to involve themselves in these arguments. This does not mean that two brawling children who are physically injuring each other should not be separated. It does mean that parents should be wary of taking sides, of getting caught up in the merits of a given argument. Left to their own devices, most children will come to some sort of understanding with each other. Also, parents should not try to dignify the children's disputes by giving them too much time and attention. The child who recognizes that fights with other children are an effective attention-getting device will only be encouraged to fight more often.

There are a few things the stepparent can do to reduce the level of tension and conflict among stepsiblings. First, if possible, children who are not used to sharing a bedroom should not be forced to share one. Given today's housing squeeze, however, the average family probably can't give every child his own room.

Even so, it is possible to give every child his own *time*. The biological parent should conscientiously strive not to favor "his own" children over his stepchildren. But he can acknowledge the specialness of his relationship with his biological child. This is best done by setting a definite period of time, preferably every day, for the biological parent and child to be alone and apart from other pressures of the household.

As time passes, the stepfamily's life together should acquire a valuable bond: that is, time itself. At the outset, the stepfamily is something of an artificial unit. Stepsiblings, in particular, are apt to feel this way; after all, *they*, unlike the adults involved, have not experienced the love and friendship that led to the remarriage of their biological parent. At the beginning children are more apt to feel the *differences* that exist between them and their stepsiblings, and to minimize the things they might have in common.

In the biological family, as we have mentioned, children grow up and *into* their family's history. From the time these children are toddlers they hear the stories that will form the family's own treasure-trove of "family mythology." Stepfamilies, too, can build a historical nest of sorts, though its growth won't be so easy and automatic as that of the biological family. Still, shared experiences and adventures can become a bond for the stepfamily. The parents can encourage development of this level of emotional life, by being aware of occasions that the family is likely to *enjoy* sharing. Areas of common interest are the key here: short trips to exciting places, vacations at a new summer house never before shared by any family members, a new pet — these may become enjoyable experiences shared uniquely by the entire stepfamily.

There is, however, no way to force these common experiences to be successful. Common emotional bonds are formed over a period of years rather than months. Patience and optimism are the important helpers here, as they are for so many other areas in the life of a stepfamily.

One obvious possibility, often spoken of as a way of "bringing the stepfamily together," is the birth of a new child, the biological child of the parent/stepparent marriage. Some parents, indeed, see this as an almost automatic way to "seal" the stepfamily and bring it to a new level of intimacy, sharing, and mutual understanding. In fact, a new baby may or may not prove a positive experience for its stepbrothers and stepsisters; it depends a very great deal on the emotional temperature of the family when the child is born. Certainly a new baby is no panacea for a troubled stepfamily, any more than it is for any troubled marriage.

Generally speaking, if your children feel coolness or animosity toward their stepparent or stepsibling, a new child may be received with similar coolness or animosity. It really is, in the children's view, a classic case of whether the glass is half full or half empty. In other words, if the stepfamily sees itself as "we" — a single workable unit — then the baby will be seen as "ours." If the stepfamily is emotionally fragmented between "us" and "them," then the baby is likely to be seen as "theirs." If a stepchild feels insecure about her place in the family, a new infant may pose yet another threat to the stepchild's relationship with his biological parent; it may be taken as another sign that the biological parent is abandoning his "old" child to take on a new family.

Obviously, the stepfamily is a very complicated organism. Stepfamilies vary enormously in terms of emotional cohesion, mutual dependence, and "family feeling" of an affectionate nature. These differences are not the differences between right and wrong; they are only the natural, understandable differences that occur among different groups of individuals attempting to share a home, or a life. When mutual respect and tolerance exist, some level of affection is likely to follow. With those three qualities, the stepfamily can build an emotional life together.

9

When and Where to Get Professional Help

CHILDREN VARY ENORMOUSLY in their ability to accept and adjust to significant change in their lives. Inevitably, some children find themselves unable to satisfactorily sort out their new circumstances and live with the reality of their parents' divorce.

Almost inevitably, when a child shows evidence of emotional problems, learning disturbances, or other signs of acute stress, parents blame themselves. It is true, as we have stressed throughout this book, that excessive parental conflict and tension can adversely affect the child. But the true reasons for a child's emotional problems are never simple or obvious. They may be and often are the result of complicated relationships among family members over a substantial period of time. The problem may also be complicated by a biochemical, organic, or physical component, such as a learning disorder.

There is no point in punishing yourself with excessive guilt if your child shows signs of emotional or behavioral problems. The important thing is to get the child appropriate professional help. Since the family is a unit, with each member's behavior affecting the others, the entire family will often have to become involved in the treatment plan.

We have already described the sometimes troubling reactions that the child may experience during the divorce period, many of which are alarming to parents. The most important question is: When is my child's behavior no longer normal? When is it advisable to seek professional help?

As a general rule, a child's behavior becomes a source of legitimate concern when she is no longer able to function normally in her daily life, or when, as with alcohol or other drug abuse, she becomes dangerously self-destructive. Thus, if your child suddenly becomes unable to function at school, if she abandons her friends and withdraws into solitude, if she consistently engages in bullying or delinquent behavior, you should not "wait it out" in hope that the problem will solve itself. These behavior patterns are strong indications that your child is suffering. Nor should you feel, as all too many parents do, that you are somehow stigmatizing the child by seeking psychological help. Such feelings are really the fantasies of the parent, and another expression of his sense of guilt. The day is long gone, fortunately, when psychiatry was known as the province of "crazies" or wealthy eccentrics. Nearly all churches, schools, and social groups today recognize the value of sound psychological counseling.

It is true that your concern over your child's behavior may be exaggerated because of your guilty feelings about the divorce. There are also parents who, also for reasons of guilt, actually minimize the seriousness of their child's problems. My advice is this: If you are, for whatever reason, seriously concerned about your child's welfare, you should resolve your concern by arranging to consult with a qualified child psychiatrist or psychologist. After appropriate evaluation, he or she will either decide that your fears are unfounded or work with your child to overcome her difficulty. Either way, both you and your child will benefit; a child, after all, can be made very anxious by a parent who is himself troubled or overanxious.

To whom should the parents go for competent professional

evaluation and counseling? There are several different types of professionals active in this field, and it might be good to note the differences among them.

A *psychiatrist* is a trained medical doctor who, after medical school, has done at least three years of further specialized training in the field of psychiatric medicine. A psychiatrist may be associated with a hospital or clinic and may also be in private practice. A psychiatrist, as a physician, is the only mental health professional who is legally entitled to write prescriptions for medication (such as tranquilizers) if he thinks they are needed.

A *child psychiatrist* is a doctor who, in addition to her years of general psychiatric training, has undergone at least two further years of specialized training in the psychology of children. A psychiatrist or child psychiatrist may also be *Board Certified*. A doctor is *Board Certified* in her specialty if, after her residency, she has undertaken further study and passed a stringent examination.

A *clinical psychologist* is not a doctor. He has, instead, a Ph.D. in psychology. This degree is awarded after approximately five years of postgraduate study and intensive training. The clinical psychologist may offer counseling or therapy identical to that offered by a psychiatrist. The psychologist, however, may not prescribe medication of any sort.

Another professional who may offer counseling or therapy is the *psychiatric social worker*. Ordinarily, the psychiatric social worker has a graduate degree (a Master of Social Work or M.S.W.) obtained after a two-year course of graduate study and training. After further experience, the psychiatric social worker may qualify to become a member of the American Council of Social Workers. Then, the initials "A.C.S.W." may appear after his or her name. The psychiatric social worker may be particularly helpful in aiding the family with concrete problems — such as economic hardship or family illness — that are contributing to the child's troubles. Ordinarily, he or she will be familiar with social agencies that aid families with these types of problems. Like the psychiatrist and the psychologist, the psychiatric social worker may be in private practice or may be attached to a hospital or clinic.

One very real difference among these three professionals lies in the area of fees. While these expenses vary geographically, ordinarily a psychiatrist will be more expensive than a psychologist or social worker. However, I must stress that, in all large and middle-size cities and increasingly in rural areas, mental health clinics do exist that offer high-quality services based on the family's ability to pay. One need not be wealthy to obtain good psychiatric care; "sliding-scale" fees, based on family income, are offered by a number of clinics and some private practitioners.

Where can you go to find a therapist who is genuinely qualified? This is an important question, because in some states professional licensing laws are loose or nonexistent. Sometimes individuals who are clearly incompetent or lacking any professional training advertise themselves as "therapists." But proper psychological help depends absolutely on proper knowledge, training, and experience. Be sure that the therapist in whom you place your trust and your child's welfare is properly qualified to render help.

I suggest, as one reliable way of locating a qualified professional, that you call your local chapter of the American Medical Association, the American Psychological Association, or the American Council of Social Workers and request a list of qualified practitioners in your area. Make sure you get more than one name, as you may well want to interview more than one possible therapist. Also, if there is a medical school in or near your city, the Department of Psychiatry is an excellent source of references. Often, too, medical schools are associated with psychiatric clinics that provide quality care.

There are other sources of information and help. Regional

Mental Health Clinics, publicly funded, now exist in many sections of the country. These centers exist precisely to provide help for troubled families and individuals.

You may also turn to those in the helping professions whom you know and whose opinion you respect. Your parish priest, minister, or rabbi, your family physician, your child's teacher or guidance counselor — such people are commonly called upon by troubled people and very often will be able to refer them to qualified, sympathetic counselors. Of course, if you think that your doctor or clergyman or your child's teacher is basically hostile to the notion of professional psychiatric help, or if you want to keep from them the fact that you are seeking such help, it is better to rely on the professional associations and centers mentioned above for information.

Let's assume, then, that you have acquired several possible names and have arranged for a consultation (which usually varies from one to three hours) with the first person on the list. When you meet this individual, by what standards should you judge him? What should you look for in a therapist?

First of all, remember that, in consulting a mental health professional, you are searching for — and paying for — high-quality service. You are a consumer; you are entitled to ask questions. This, of course, should be done in a friendly and straightforward manner. Feel free to ask the professional about his education and training, his years of experience, his areas of expertise, and about such practical matters as fees and payment schedules.

The consultation may be done in one or more sessions. The therapist will want to see you and your child separately, and he may want to talk to you together.

What should you expect from a consultation? My feeling is that, at least after several sessions with a child, the psychiatrist or psychologist should be able to: (1) provide a careful assessment of the nature of the child's psychological difficulties; (2)

listen carefully to the child, allowing her ample opportunities to express her feelings or beliefs; (3) communicate to the child that he understands her and wishes to be of help; (4) define for you in some way the purposes or goals of the therapy. A therapist who can accomplish these far-from-easy tasks is, to my mind, competent, sensitive, and practical.

One other factor in evaluating psychiatrists or psychologists should also be mentioned, although it should be obvious. That is, you should trust your own instincts about the basic character of the therapist to whom you are entrusting your child. You should feel, after an hour or two of conversation, that you are dealing with a sensitive, interested, trustworthy person of sound judgment. If a psychiatrist, however exalted his professional credentials, seems to be basically cold, remote, and rigid, then probably he is not the person to treat your child.

I must alert you, however, to a possible complication here. That is, you should be on guard against those feelings in yourself that might arise against *any* psychiatrist or psychologist. Even though you may rationally realize that seeking psychological help for your child is the best course, you may half-consciously resent the fact that you are turning over your child to another adult for treatment. These feelings may intensify in the course of your child's therapy, since your child must inevitably become somewhat attached to his therapist, if the therapy is to be successful. Be aware that you may experience feelings of jealousy and even hostility toward your child's therapist, which may be intensified by your feelings of guilt at having "failed" your child in the first place.

Too often, in fact, a parent will suddenly take his child out of therapy just as the child seems to be improving. This is usually due to the parent's jealousy toward the therapist, who now shares his child's affection and trust. Sometimes, too, it becomes clear that the child's "illness" really serves some unconscious need of the parent. On some deep level, then, the parent resents the fact that his child is no longer ill.

This is one example of the ways in which the *relationship* and *interaction* between parent and child can lie at the root of the child's problem. In other words, the unhealthy symptoms of the child are mirrored in the emotional troubles of the parent.

In such cases, the child's psychologist may recommend that the parent, too, enter therapy. Not infrequently, the parent reacts to this suggestion with anger or embarrassment. Such feelings are misplaced. You are not being accused of being "sick" or of deliberately harming your child. I urge you, if the suggestion is made, to sincerely explore the possibility of entering therapy yourself. After all, an exploratory session or two with a sympathetic professional can hardly do anyone any harm.

When we speak generally of "therapy" what do we mean? In the adult context, there are almost innumerable forms of therapy derived from many different theories of psychology.

In the case of children, generally, the *forms* of therapy, at least, are simpler. For part of the time at least, the therapist will simply converse with your child, encouraging her to reveal her true thoughts and feelings. At some point, usually at the outset, the therapist may administer one or more psychological tests to your child, to help him accurately diagnose the child's problems. The child may also participate in *group therapy*, which is designed to teach her to relate in a healthy, satisfying way to other children. This may be particularly helpful if the child has displayed social problems such as excessive shyness or bullying behavior toward other children.

Play therapy is widely utilized with children and has been shown to be particularly effective. Play therapy is just what the name implies: The therapist provides the child with certain toys, including dolls, a doll house, and so on, and asks the child to "tell a story" using the toys. Almost always, the child's games reveal a great deal about his feelings toward and relationships with important people in his life. In this nonthreatening way, the therapist can learn a great deal about the child's situation. Very often, when one child shows symptoms of emotional distress, it indicates that the family as a *unit* is in distress. In many such cases, it is best if the entire family is able to discuss and examine its relationship together. *Family therapy* enables them to do this. In family therapy, all family members (except the noncustodial parent) meet with the therapist. By engaging in discussion relating to family members, the therapist can observe the patterns of behavior in the family, watching how one family member relates to another. Often it develops that it is the *pattern* of family relationships that is unhealthy, rather than the emotional state of any one individual. Family therapy can be very intense, and many parents are frankly nervous about displaying family secrets before the therapist. Parents should remember, however, that professional psychiatrists and psychologists are experienced in dealing with family secrets. They are unlikely to be surprised or shocked by anything they hear in family therapy. If your child's therapist genuinely feels that family therapy is the best choice for your family's happiness, parents should put aside any misguided or self-protective feelings of embarrassment or hostility and make a sincere attempt to participate.

Professional therapy, then, is often necessary and can be enormously helpful to the child and the entire family. Parents who are facing the social, financial, and emotional stress following divorce, however, can also look to other nonprofessional organizations for help. These groups, consisting of divorced and other single parents facing similar problems, can offer a great deal of practical advice and emotional support to the divorced parent.

"Parents Without Partners" is one such organization, which I recommend highly. This group now has chapters in most cities.

In addition, many churches, social centers, and civic organizations now run their own divorce "self-help" groups or can refer the parent to such a group.

It can be extremely helpful for a newly divorced or separated parent to meet with other sympathetic people in the same situation. Among other things, it helps to remove that horrible sense of isolation often felt by the newly single parent left with the problems and responsibilities of raising children alone.

Obviously, this book cannot describe every possible problem that the divorced parent may face. Individual situations vary widely. I intended here, in these short pages, to explain generally the way your child thinks and the emotional and intellectual understanding that he will bring to the reality of divorce. I suggested approaches that you could use to minimize the trauma that your child might otherwise experience.

I believe that with love, knowledge, and patience you can ease the inevitable tensions and distress of the divorce period for your child. In doing that, you will have avoided many of the most painful complications you yourself would otherwise have to undergo. Finally, if it develops that your child needs professional help, you will again be making things easier for both yourself and your child.

I fully appreciate that this is not an easy time for you. I know that you deeply love and are concerned for the welfare of your children. I hope that this book has been at least a starting point to help you through this draining and complicated time. Good luck.